Praise for *The Father You Get*

"Is this that book about what a great father you think you are?"
—**Lou Dodd**

"I'm going to write a book about all the things you left out."
—**Henry Dodd**

"I'm not sure memoirs are ethical."
—**Bel Dodd**

"With the eloquence of a poet and the unflinching honesty of a man who has wrestled with his own story, Dodd delivers a poignant memoir about fatherhood, grace, and the long shadow of a painful past. This book is a gift to anyone who has ever wondered if they are doomed to repeat the past or if transformation and redemption are truly possible. Read this book. Let it change you."
—**Ian Morgan Cron**, coauthor of *The Road Back to You: An Enneagram Journey to Self-Discovery*

"I love my dad with my whole heart, but we have a deeply complicated relationship. Which is to say, we're like most fathers and sons. Patton Dodd's story is not my story exactly, but reading it felt strangely familiar in parts and helped me better understand my own. *The Father You Get* is a brave book and a riveting exploration of the nature of the relationships between parent and child—both the ones that actually exist and the ones we often fantasize about. I could not stop turning the pages of this honest, insightful memoir. Everyone who has a father should read it—and yes, that means all of us."

—**Jonathan Merritt**, author of *Learning to Speak God from Scratch: Why Sacred Words Are Vanishing—and How We Can Revive Them*

"This extraordinary book is a rare blend of raw honesty, unexpected humor, and unflinching self-reflection. Patton Dodd takes us on a journey through the stories that shape us—the ones we inherit, the ones we misunderstand, and the ones we must ultimately rewrite. He allows us to experience the long arc of reckoning, the tension between anger and compassion, as he achieves the nearly impossible balancing act of holding grief and gratitude in the same hand. Beautifully written and deeply affecting, this book is about learning how to see—our pasts, our parents, our children, and ourselves… and it will stay with you long after you turn the last page."

—**Nancy French**, New York Times bestselling author

"*The Father You Get* is a book for the haunted and the hopeful—for those shaped by absence and longing for presence. In this masterclass in how to write honestly, Dodd shows how excavating a father's hidden truths is an act of redemption (for past, present, and future). The weight of the topic is naturally heavy, but often relieved by humor and top-shelf, compact writing. For anyone who has ever looked back to move forward, this is a book for you."

—**Charlie Peacock**, Grammy Award–winning music producer and author of *Roots and Rhythm: A Life in Music*

"*The Father You Get* is a stirring meditation on what it means to need and become the many things we expect of fathers: a parent, a mentor, a hero, a friend. With abiding warmth and humor, Patton Dodd's engaging memoir captures the poignancy of trying to be all we wish we'd had."

—**Peter Manseau**, author of *The Apparitionists*

"What to do when you are dead set on not becoming the father you got? Take a road trip to dig up dirt on a deadbeat covered head to toe in it, reckon with his drunken neglect without prettying it up, and set it all down in indelible prose that exposes your own fatherly insecurities alongside the saving grace of your mother. A high-wire act of a 'my-damn-dad' memoir shuttling between anger and acceptance, doubt and faith."

—**Stephen Prothero**, author of *God Is Not One: The Eight Rival Religions That Run the World—and Why Their Differences Matter*

THE FATHER YOU GET

THE FATHER YOU GET
AND THE ONES YOU MAKE, BELIEVE IN, AND BECOME

PATTON DODD

Broadleaf Books
Minneapolis

THE FATHER YOU GET
And the Ones You Make, Believe In, and Become

Copyright © 2025 Patton Dodd. Published in association with Pape Commons, www.papecommons.com. Published by Broadleaf Books. All rights reserved. Except for brief quotations in critical articles or reviews, no part of this book may be reproduced in any manner without prior written permission from the publisher. Email copyright@broadleafbooks.com or write to Permissions, Broadleaf Books PO Box 1209, Minneapolis, MN 55440-1209.

30 29 28 27 26 25   1 2 3 4 5 6 7 8 9

Library of Congress Control Number: 2024060208 (print)

Cover image: © 2024 Getty Images; Middle-aged man/183355550 by DNY59; Paper by obsidian too on Unsplash
Cover design: Gabe Nansen

Print ISBN: 978-1-5064-8698-7
eBook ISBN: 978-1-5064-8699-4

Printed in India

For Michaela, Bel, Henry, and Lou

CONTENTS

Acknowledgments — ix
Preface: Make Me a Man — xiii

Part 1
The Father I Got

1. This Guy Sucks — 3
2. Where to Begin? — 17
3. The Lawn Mower — 27
4. Missing the Obvious — 39
5. The Legend of Bill Dodd — 55

Part 2
The Ones You Make

6. Papa Friend — 71
7. Lord, Make Me Some Men — 79
8. The Pastor — 93
9. Figure Out — 107

Part 3
The One You Believe in

10. Father God, Giver of Bikes — 123
11. Faith Is a Faucet — 129
12. Mom's Life of Prayer — 133

13. Father in Heaven, Mother on Earth   143
14. The Years the Locusts Ate   153
15. The Addiction Expert   165

Part 4
The One You Become

16. The Story Machine   177
17. Why Dads Are So Cheesy   187
18. Dad Lessons   197
19. The Future of Fatherhood   213

ACKNOWLEDGMENTS

FIFTEEN OR SO years ago at a conference in Philadelphia, I met up with a new friend, Lil Copan, who worked in publishing. She asked if I had any book ideas, and I pitched a concept that had come to me the day before: *FourFathers*, a memoir of my dad, father figures, God the Father, and being a father.

Even as I pitched it, I knew I didn't want to write it just yet. Thinking a lot about my dad, for starters, was not something I was ready to do.

Four years ago, I sent Lil and Broadleaf Books a different book proposal, which they rejected. "But hey," she said. "I always liked the *FourFathers* idea. When are you going to write that?"

This book exists because of Lil—her attention and her memory.

Also, Don Pape, who has shepherded this project from the beginning and long been a source of good counsel and good vibes.

Broadleaf Books is a gem. Andrew DeYoung's editorial embrace was just what I needed—I overhauled everything based on his good questions. (He was also very, very patient.) Lisa Eaton is a project management pro, and Janna Green is a copyediting pro.

My colleagues and friends at the H. E. Butt Foundation gave me the right kind of space during this project, asking *howzit goin* but also letting it be the personal side hustle it very much was. I'm grateful to many people in that organization, especially David and Deborah Rogers.

Alice Rhee never let a conversation go by without asking why I wasn't writing more. John Garland pumped his fist about this project—and helped me see that the lawn mower story was central. Elizabeth Coffee restored my self-confidence when I had reached new lows. Ryan Lugalia-Hollon asked questions that suggested direction. Mark Menjivar kept reminding me—and modeling for me—how much acts of creation matter.

Mark Steele buoyed my spirits (and several of my sentences). Peder Halseide kept things strange and true, as ever. Perri Rosheger got real with me and believed in me. Andrew Schmidt told me to own what was mine to own. Marcus Goodyear modeled how to learn from one's own children. Anne Snyder strengthened my sense of what this book is for. So did Shannon Hopkins, on multiple occasions, along with placing it in a broader context I needed to envision.

Dianne Garcia helped me look past my insecurities and even my failures. She is the living embodiment of the *keep going* principle.

John Bolin affirmed my intentions and offered leeway. Carolyn Garza got me over a key mental-spiritual block, and not for the first time. Steven Purcell told me, in more ways than he knew, that my voice could be trusted.

Rob Stennett is the Nikola Jokic of creative counsel—the right assist at the right time—and the Jamal Murray of clutch conversations. Brandon Shupp let me bend his ear—he was the first audience of the stories about my mom. He used to say that I was the one who did all the listening in our long friendship, but that's not true.

John Diliberto, Matt Diliberto, and Carlos Trujillo were there way back when, and they still are there across time and distance. Roger Sandberg, Bill Townsend, and Ryan O'Neal are proof positive that even sporadic communication can be sustaining.

Tara Owens, *anam cara*—gosh, I don't even know how to say what she was and is for me and for this project. That is a whole other book.

I have near-daily conversation partners—in my head, and in my inbox—in Wilson Brissett, Matt Burnett, Jeff Culver, Jim Knutsen, B.J. Strawser, and Glenn Paauw. Much of the best stuff that roams around in my mind each day comes from them.

I listened to an enormous amount of Waxahatchee while writing this book. Katie Crutchfield's lyrics are both poetic and plainspoken, and when I was not sure how to put something, it was often a Waxahatchee song that helped me tell the truth in the way I wanted to tell the truth.

Of course, key sections of this book were made possible by people who shared time and stories with me. Such sharing is an act of mercy. Thank you to Quincy, David, Karen, Mike, Beth, Hannah, Carter, Jack, Beverly, Kenny, BJ, and especially to Me-Me.

As for Kaysie—well, it's tough to limit myself to a sentence or two in acknowledgment of such love, devotion, wisdom, and courage. She takes up a lot of room in my heart, as does her beloved family.

As for my own family—Michaela, Bel, Henry, and Lou, I wrote this book for you. I mean you as a whole, but also each of you individually. Each of you is a unique wonder to me. This book is a testament to the education in love that our lives together have been and will continue to be. I am overjoyed that you are the family I got.

PREFACE

MAKE ME A MAN

IT IS FIVE o'clock and almost hot on a mid-May evening in San Antonio, Texas. I am standing in a crowding bar near downtown—not crowd*ed* just yet, but it's about to be. People are pouring in and the server is inking her notepad with orders. I am holding a self-serve cup of water and talking to a man I have met just moments before.

And much to this man's dismay, I am starting to cry.

I mention the water because I want you to know that is the only thing I've yet had to drink—the tears have nothing to do with any foreign substance in my system. I am helping throw a goodbye party for one of my dearest friends, a woman named Alice whom everyone loves and whose party is the reason the bar is crowding at five o'clock sharp. Friends arrive on time in honor of Alice, for whom being five minutes early is being ten minutes late. I am busy greeting everyone and making sure our reserved area is arranged just so, and—again—I've not even had a chance to order a drink.

The man I have just met is named Dan, a friend of Alice's from one of her many walks of life. We shake hands and I ask him if he is from San Antonio.

"Nope," he says. "Born and raised in New York City. I moved here for work three years ago. How about you? Where are you from?"

Now, there's a question. It's a version of the same one I asked him. It's the most normal question for just-meeting humans to ask each other. But whenever I'm asked it, I take a beat to gather my thoughts.

I've developed a few strategies in handling *Where are you from?* Sometimes I just say "Colorado." That's good enough, because I lived there during middle school, high school, and a portion of my college years, then again for a couple of adult stretches of life. But it always feels a bit off to me. I'm not *from* Colorado, if *from* means *where you were born*. I am *from* Nashville, Tennessee. But my family left Nashville when I was one year old. For a while we lived in Jackson, Tennessee, changing homes a time or three. Then Alabama, then Northern California, with more home- and neighborhood- and school district hopping in each of those places. We also had frequent visits and a couple of long stays in northern Mississippi. After high school, I started my own peripatetic path: Tulsa, then back to Colorado—Fort Collins, then Colorado Springs—and then Boston—Belmont, then Southie—then back to Colorado again, then northern Maryland, and finally San Antonio, where, at forty years old, I landed with my own young family and an intention to plant roots.

So. The question is how to answer the question. I feel like I should tell the truth. Only I don't know what the truth is.

Sometimes I just say, "Kind of all over." Then people do one of two things. They smile and nod and move things right along, or they say, "Oh, military family?"

Standing in the crowding bar, Dan chooses the second route.

"Was your dad in the military?"

"No, he just changed jobs a lot," I reply. I look around for that server.

"Oh? Was he an entrepreneur?"

This is one I hadn't heard before. I pause, then say, "He was . . . uh, I dunno. We just moved around." I figure that would be the end of it, but no. Alice's friend is a persistent man.

"But why? Traveling salesman?" he says, smirking. "Was he always being headhunted or something?"

This guy. He's being cute, I suppose. I decide to be cute right back.

"No," I say. "He was a drunk. He'd drink his way out of jobs, burn bridges, and we'd have to go someplace new."

And then I—someone who that night was in a grand mood, and someone who would have told you he did not feel all that burdened by his troubled childhood—promptly burst into tears.

I raise a "Give me a minute" finger. I try to smile, but my face refuses. More tears come. A friend comes up to say hi, sees me crying, then furrows his brow and turns to poor Dan, who goes ashen with guilt.

I gather myself. I tell Dan I am sorry and that it had been a long day. I excuse myself and go to the bathroom. I collect my emotions and go back into the fray, making sure Alice has the send-off she deserves.

Dan and I do a good job of avoiding each other the rest of the night.

• • •

We lived in all kinds of places: subsidized housing, low-end apartments, a duplex, a home we owned until the first bankruptcy, split-level rentals, houses we borrowed from our fellow churchgoers in one Southern Baptist church or another. "Y'all were always on the move," my cousin Beverly remembered as she drove me around Jackson on a recent trip and showed me the remains of one of the neighborhoods my family had passed through.

When I was eight, we moved into a gargantuan red brick house in an affluent neighborhood in Huntsville, Alabama. The homeowners had decided to be missionaries overseas for a year, and for that year their home was made available to us. I'm not sure who this family was and there is no one around who can tell me, but I remember feeling surrounded by the strange, wonderful aura of their wealth. I slept in another boy's bed and played with another boy's toys. I enjoyed his toys some but not as much as the fact that the family had left their TV cable subscription on. For a year, I watched *Belle and Sebastian* on repeat, along with all the *You Can't Do That on Television* and Nick at Nite I could handle, and with Dad always . . . somewhere, Mom preoccupied with Dad, and my teenage sister, Kaysie, always out with friends, I could handle a lot of it.

In my second semester of fourth grade, we moved into another borrowed house, this one a single story on a small hill with a wide, busy street in front. We were there but a couple of months, long enough to acquire a gray kitten named Misty who lived with us for a bit and then must have found her own place. Next, we moved all the way to Northern California, where for a few weeks we stayed in a small yellow house, all our moving boxes packed and stacked around us because we were told we would not be there for long. We moved into another temporary house for a bit, then into a second-story apartment that was big enough for everyone but me to have a bedroom. I slept on the couch that year, falling asleep while Dad watched *Monday Night Football* or *Miami Vice*. I didn't complain about the couch, and maybe that's why in the couple of moves after that, Mom gave me bedroom dibs.

Unless we were living in borrowed homes with other people's furniture and fixings, Mom decorated each home the same way—the same family photo collages, the same magnolia tree paintings, the same crocheted Bible verses in wooden frames.

Of these constants, the one I remember most was a framed poem written by my father. Whenever we moved, I'd always look to see where Mom had placed it. Prominent positions sometimes, other times relegated to my parent's bedroom. By the time I was in high school in Colorado Springs, it hung in the half-basement family room, tucked away in a corner where hardly anyone ever had occasion to turn their eyes. At Christmastime, the tree was positioned right in front of it.

At some point the poem went into a cardboard box, which is where it has sat until a few months ago, when I pulled it out of my attic here in Texas, undid its old newspaper wrapping, and read it for the first time in a couple of decades.

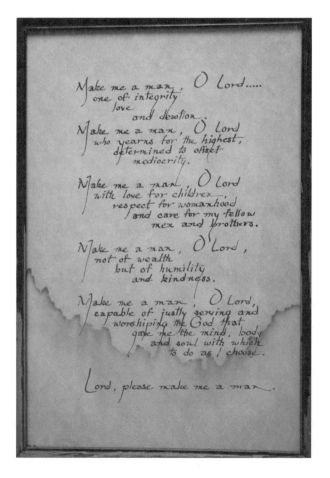

That frame and the waterlogged paper it holds date back, I assume, to the 1970s. It might be as old as I am, getting close to its half-century mark.

I majored in English, then went to graduate school for religion and literature. I spent several years teaching composition to college students. I mention those bona fides only to say to you: Look, I recognize this is not a good poem. It doesn't scan; it's sentimental and baggy; it's just a prayer written in verse.

But to me, throughout my childhood, "Make Me a Man" was also a fascinating story, and one that was hard to believe. One day, a young-man version of my father, full of feeling, sat down with a pen and focused on those feelings. He reflected on what he wanted in life, who he wanted to be. He captured those reflections in language. He wrote up a prayer for a life well lived. He showed his work to my mom, maybe reading it aloud to her in his caramel Southern drawl. My mom was moved enough by my father's prayer-poem to have it done up in calligraphy, printed on pretty paper, and put into this slim frame.

She hung the poem from home to home. And in each of those homes, my father walked past the poem every day. And on each of those days, he proceeded to make sure that his prayer was being answered with a clear, resounding *nah*.

• • •

This book is a memoir of the fathers I've had and pursued and tried to be. I'd planned it as a series of reflections on fatherhood based on my stories, but the stories took over the whole thing. The stories are the reflections.

If we don't know our backstory—if no one ever told it to us, if we never paid attention to it, or whatever—then we have two options. We can make up fictions, living with delusions of how we got to be the way we are. Or we can start trying, through memory and contemplation and conversation, to get as close to the truth of ourselves as possible. Either way, we're all living within a story of who we are. We're not writing that story from scratch—our lives begin *in medias res*, emerging from a prehistory. The better we understand our backstory, the better chance we have of writing our way forward into a story we want to live.

My story begins with my dad, a troubled man who caused a lot of trouble for pretty much everyone who ever got close to him. He spent his life hiding, and our lives were the consequences of that hiding. A father's secrets about who he is can become his children's inheritance, shaping not only how they see him but also how they see themselves.

Like a lot of people, I lived with a dad-shaped hole in my life, one I tried to fill with other dad-like people—mentors and pastors and friends and strangers. I went on a long and winding search for father figures. As you'll see, parts of my search were pretty silly, pretty misguided. Yet I contend that if you need fathering, you can go out there and find it—but you best be honest with yourself and with the people you're taking the fathering from.

After I wrote of father figures, I'd intended to narrate my bumbling search for God the Father, but my mom took over that part of the story. That's because the best way I know to contemplate God is to consider my mom's faith—a big, thick, pained, active faith that she labored to hand off to me. I suspect I'm in good company here—the world is full of people whose belief in God the Father persists because of their mother.

Eventually, I became a father, and I soon learned that becoming a father is not something that happens when a kid is born. A father forms over time—it's an ongoing education, and even though I've been at it for more than two decades, my education is yet underway. If I'm lucky, I'll keep learning to be a father for the rest of my life.

Universal truths—the meanings of life we share with each other—become clear only through particulars. Each of us is an instance of our whole. I trust my particular story of the fathers I got, made, believed in, and became has something to say to you about yours.

Part 1

THE FATHER I GOT

For the more haunted among us, only looking back at the past can permit it finally to become past.

—Mary Karr

Anything true can be talked about.

—Matt Burnett

1

This Guy Sucks

I'VE SPENT MUCH of my life nursing incuriosity about my father, a shovel of a man who dug his family into deeper and deeper holes. He was a drunk. Later, he added a drug addiction. He practiced insolvency, looking for handouts and conniving his way through life. He was passed out on the couch pretty much every night of my life. He moved us around the country without much of a plan or purpose.

Some families suffer through hardship together, but for us Dad *was* the hardship—stubborn in his addictions, persistent in his negligence. He was the one predictable, dependable fact of our uncertain lives, even as we lived those lives in the constant hope that he would change.

Why was he the way he was? That was the biggest mystery. Dad was unknowable—that's one thing he was very good at. Ask my father questions about his upbringing, and he'd bob and weave. Wonder aloud about his family of origin, and he'd grin-grimace and leave the room, like you'd let out a nasty fart. He refused to go deep with anyone in his life. Even my mom professed to know little of the backstory of the man she married and worried over for four decades.

For a while in my college years, I pressed into the void. I wanted to fill in the outline of my father. I invited him to the movies and took him to lunch when I was home visiting. But he blocked and disappointed me at every pass—and passed out during some of our outings together. It felt like Dad had to drink extra hard in order to get ready to hang out with me. So, I resolved to a studied indifference. My heart's embers cooled, and I didn't stoke them. I decided I'd just as soon be free of him. As I got older, the lack of stories, the black hole of information, made him thinner, lighter, easier to slip.

Dad was still in our lives some after my sister and I were grown up and gone to our respective cities—me to Fort Collins, Colorado Springs, and Boston; Kaysie to Tulsa. Mom would come visit us in those places, and we loved it when she came solo. But sometimes Dad would tag along, and we'd have to deal with him. When Kaysie and I married our spouses and started having kids, Dad became "Papa," and there are pictures of him holding our babies and smiling over them in the late '90s and early '00s. Thanksgiving and Christmas meant being stuck with him, but I became skilled at minimizing our interactions as much as possible. We small-talked our way through the years, the Denver Broncos and Boston Red Sox becoming the full range of our conversation.

Of course, we could not shrink-fit Dad entirely. We could not tuck him away, especially as long as he and Mom stayed married. He was always the focus of pained conversation with her, as Kaysie and I encouraged her to go to Al-Anon, seek counsel, find an exit ramp, get the hell out. Mom finally left him in early 2007. By the time Dad died later that year, he did not exist for us as our father so much as a heavy, bothersome weight we dragged behind us. His death allowed us to release the grip.

Mourn him? I didn't even miss him.

Whole weeks passed where I hardly gave him a thought, though I did have pangs of guilt for feeling free at last. For months after he died, friends would say, "I was so sorry to hear about your father," and I would think, "That's because you haven't really heard about him."

Dad was a ghost even while he was alive. In death, he was a vapor.

One late spring a decade or so ago, I went on a camping trip with a bunch of guys. We ended up talking about our dads around the campfire. Well, *they* ended up talking about *their* dads. I could not think of any tales to tell. No sob stories I felt like sharing. No good anecdotes. I just could not think of anything at all to say about the man. I'd shaped my heart into a vacuum of him. Indifference was bliss.

And yet. The older you get, the more willing you become to accept that some things are true whether you want them to be or not.

I look a good bit like my dad, and every now and then the mirror reminds me that I'm his son. His curly hair grew into thin tufts as he aged; mine is doing the same. Dad used to grunt as he stood up and grunt again as he sat down; I've started doing that too. He also grunted as he ate, which was always an issue of peak annoyance for me—I could hardly stand to sit through meals with the man. The other night, one of my kids asked me why I grunt while I eat. (*Dammit.*) Dad used to dart his eyes around the room while you talked to him—not out of avoidance so much as just a weird twitch. The last couple of years, I've caught my eyes dancing about.

I could simply refuse to be like him. I could deny his presence in my body, my bank account, my imagination about the world. But that tends to be a recipe for becoming what you resent.

• • •

One afternoon last summer, I headed to a restaurant with my wife and two of our kids—Henry and Louisa, 16 and 13, respectively, at the time. Right as I was trying to pull our car into a tight parking space a couple of blocks away, Louisa said something to me from the back seat. I heard her but didn't respond because I was focused on what I was doing. She said it again, and this time I heard her a bit less—I knew she was saying something, but I was doing the thing I was doing. She said it again, her voice a website buried twenty tabs over.

Once I had the car parked but while we were still inside it, I was thinking about where we were in relationship to where we were going and the fact that I needed to find the pay station for parking and *Oh crap, look at that, my phone is almost out of battery* and other spare thoughts tumbling around my brain.

Meanwhile, Lou was still trying to get my attention from the back seat. "Dad . . . Dad . . . Dad! DAD!"

I snapped: "Lou, *hold on*! I need you to be patient!" In my mind, it was a snap of justified frustration: She was ignoring what I was doing and focused on only whatever small thing she wanted. She needed to learn to wait.

My wife, Michaela, saw different. "Hold on," she said from the shotgun seat. "She's been talking to you and you haven't responded." ("Yeah, Dad," said Lou.)

I turned and looked first at Michaela, then at Lou. "That's because I'm concentrating," I said. "I need her to wait when I'm focusing on something."

"Then tell her that instead of just ignoring her," said Michaela.

"I didn't ignore her!"

"You *did*. You do this a lot." (Another "Yeah, Dad" from Lou.)

My wife was at her level best here—not snapping or sniping, just pointing out what was obvious to everyone else in the car. On many days I'd have argued my point further, thanks to an instinctual conviction that Dad Has a Point is a higher principle than Whatever the Kid Needs. Or, worse, I would have argued out of sheer defensive frustration. Like most people, I'm a machine made of my habits. Like most people, I need a mechanic. Like most dads, I'm prone to dismiss the mechanics in my own family.

But on that day, in that moment, thanks be to Michaela, thanks be to God, I was able to hear the diagnosis.

Shit, I thought. *I DO do this a lot.*

I've long had a wicked case of selective hearing. There is not a number high enough to count the times someone has said something to me that goes more or less unheard—even as I am in the same room, even as I am looking right at them. My eyes might be on them, but my mind is somewhere else. But because I never ignore someone on purpose, I've had a hard time accepting blame for this problem. It's always an accident: *I was just focused on something else.* Or it's always on the other person: *Can't you see I'm focused on something else?*

But my case of selective hearing could have a cumulative effect on my kids. Maybe they'd come to think of their dad as a guy who can't be bothered. A man who would just as well ignore them. That could not be further from what I want them to believe about me. It could not be further from what I want to be true of our relationship.

I processed all this as we walked to the restaurant. Before we settled at our table, I pulled Louisa aside and apologized. I asked her if she really does feel that I ignore her a lot.

She nodded. "You do it all the time. But it's okay."

"No, it's really not okay," I said. "I'm glad I see the problem now, though. I intend to do better."

• • •

I wrote that story up a couple of weeks after it happened, then told Lou I'd done it. Her response: "Good. Now the whole entire world can go, 'This guy sucks.'"

• • •

When my father was a nineteen-year-old man serving in the National Guard, a fired gun ruptured his left eardrum, rendering it useless for the rest of his life.

Dad could hear alright with his one good ear, but his left-ear deafness combined with his own case of selective hearing. My whole life, most every interaction with him began with a string of "How's that?"—two or three at minimum, sometimes more, like a tic. At times it felt like learned behavior, as if Dad expected not to have to pay attention to your first three or four attempts to say something to him, like you were some kind of Louisa calling at him from the back seat.

Dad kept the TV volume at airplane engine levels. When I would walk through the front door and hear the blaring noise, I'd beeline for the living room to turn it down. Inevitably, Dad would be snoring in a boozy nap, but half the time he'd wake up with a jerk when the volume went down, as if the din was a blanket I'd ripped off him. "Oh wow, I went out!" he said every single time he jolted awake, as predictable as a talking doll.

"Go back to sleep, Dad," I'd mutter as I left the room.

"I think I might," he'd half say, half snore, almost out again as he said it.

We had this exact exchange four million times. It felt like needle pricks on the back of my neck.

I can remember joking with Mom and Kaysie about Dad's hearing when I was a little kid, and I even remember Dad laughing along with us a few times—his hearing loss was, at one point, something other than a source of great resentment. But as I got older, and as Dad descended further into his addictions, I lost patience. I hated his being hard of hearing. I got to where I'd say something and then repeat it right away, amplified with spite: "Dad, I need to borrow the car DAD I NEED TO BORROW THE CAR."

Then I got to where I tried to never say anything to him at all.

The memory of all this came back to me on that recent day when Louisa was trying to get my attention. And so, when I was made aware that my own selective hearing was not just a quirk but *something I do all the time*, to the deficit of my wife's and kids' feelings, it was accompanied by a crushing recognition.

I am Bill Dodd's son.

• • •

It's an admission I've been coming to for a while: I had a father. I'd prefer to pretend I didn't. He has felt like a big nothing to me for a long time, but that's a fiction. I had a dad, and he has shaped how I move through this world. He is there in the anxiety I feel most every morning, my chest tight with uncertainty about how the day is going to go. He is there at the grocery store when I shop with worry over whether we are spending too much even in the months when I have budgeted well what we can spend. He is there in all my wandering and wondering, all my insecurity and disbelief.

And then there's this surprising, pathetic truth: Sometimes I just plain miss him. When the Denver Broncos won the Super Bowl in 2016, I wanted to call Dad. When Donald Trump took the White House, I wanted to hear his reaction—I wanted to know what it would have been like to talk to him about that world-shifting event. I don't think I would have enjoyed either one of those phone calls had they actually been able to happen, but I wanted them all the same.

I know he'd be proud of some things I've done—articles I've published in some of his favorite publications, trail races I've run, countries I've had a chance to visit. He'd enjoy meals I know how to make, smacking and grunting his pleasure. He'd be impressed by the work I'm doing in Texas, and I wish he could put eyes on it.

More importantly, more tenderly, I've wished *for his sake* that he could know the wonderful grandchildren he never really had a chance to know and the ones he died too soon to meet.

I do not miss the man that Bill Dodd was. But I miss the man he could have been. I can imagine the Bill Dodd who wrote "Make Me a Man." I can imagine that man being my father. Instead, he was another man, one whose life felt too long, whose death could not come too quickly.

Still, I exist because of him. And the way that I am was shaped by his way—that's just how it is for all of us. None of us get to start from scratch. My story is folded into his story.

If I want to be a good reader of my own story, I best get to know the prequel.

• • •

On a sunny midafternoon in late April 2023, I drove a rental car into Louisville, Mississippi, with two clues about what I'd find there:

1. My dad was buried in an unmarked grave between his parents' plots in a cemetery near the town square.
2. Dad's old drinking buddy might still have been living in the area—a man named David Wilson who was also the town's recently retired municipal judge.

Dad's older cousin, Quincy, had given me these clues that very morning at his home in Tallahassee, Florida. I'd spent the night before plying Quincy with questions. Up to that point, Quincy was the only person in my dad's family who had been willing to talk to me about him. He was my first stop on a half-planned, half-not trip across the Deep South to see if I could get more people to talk.

Dad used to say that Quincy was his best friend, and Quincy agreed—"Yes, I bet he saw me that way." He told me they had spoken by phone about once a year, a general catch-up—work is fine, kids are fine, sure do miss you.

"I did love your father," Quincy told me, which makes him the only person on Earth I've ever heard say such a thing. Except for my mom, on occasion, but we'll get to her later.

When Dad died in Tulsa, Oklahoma, in 2007, Quincy reached out to my sister, Kaysie, and me to say how important it was to him that Dad's ashes be sent to Mississippi so he could see to a proper burial. At the time, I'd found the request treacly and tiresome. Why honor a man whom everyone wanted gone? Gravesites are for the living, and as far as I could tell, no one alive gave a shit about Bill Dodd.

Except Quincy—sweet, loving Quincy. Out of respect for him, we'd had the ashes shipped.

Now, sixteen years later, I was grateful for Quincy's righteous request.

I found the town square, and then the graveyard, and parked across the street. Immediately, just to the left of the entrance, I saw the tombs of Dad's parents, Elsie Rae (1906–1996) and Saffold Dodd (1900–1979), whom we knew as Big Mama and Big Daddy, respectively. In between them, Quincy told me, he had taken a shovel and buried my father's ashes.

I sat between Big Mama and Big Daddy, about where Dad must be. I plucked a few blades of grass. I looked up into the surrounding trees. I closed my eyes. I tried remembering something about Dad, feeling something of him. Nothing came. I tried talking to him—"Well, Dad, here I am." I do this with my mom on occasion. When she died in 2018, my friend Cheryl encouraged me to speak out loud to her. I found the advice just crazy enough to try, and it's been a godsend. I do it on the semi-regular, whenever I feel the urge. When I talk to Mom, I sense someone listening.

Dad, though, didn't seem to be there. My words just evaporated into the empty air. *This is so stupid*, I thought. I was an idiot full of sound and fury, signifying nothing on an unmarked grave. Dramatic but dumb. Why was I expecting anything to come of this?

Suddenly, I no longer had any interest in tracking down Quincy's second clue—Dad's drinking buddy, David Wilson. He would be hard to find, and he would likely not remember Dad anyway. I decided to hit the road. I rose from the grave (so to speak) and walked to my car.

I needed coffee, and I noticed that there was a café in the town square, just blocks away. I parked across the street from the café, got out, looked up, and realized I was standing in front of the Louisville courthouse.

Welp. If David Wilson was the retired municipal judge, he wouldn't be in there, but surely someone inside would know who he was and how to reach him. I'd come all this way. The front door was forty feet away. I guess I had to try.

Five minutes later, I had a Post-it note with David Wilson's cell phone number, no questions asked. Small towns are a wonderful thing.

I walked outside the courthouse and dialed the number. No answer. I left a voicemail.

"Hello, sir. My name is Patton Dodd, and I am the son of Bill Dodd. If that name means anything to you, I'd sure love to talk to you. Please call me if this makes any sense."

By the time I got into the car and cranked the engine, my phone rang back.

"Hello?"

"Yes, hello, this is David Wilson."

"Thank you for calling me. Did you hear my voicemail?"

"Yes, I heard it."

"So, does the name Bill Dodd mean anything to you?"

"Sure it does. I was just talking about Billy the other day."

"You were?"

"Sure I was. We talk about him all the time around here."

"You do?"

"Sure we do. Billy Dodd is a legend in this town."

2

Where to Begin?

THE FIRST TIME I went to a therapist's office, I opened by explaining that I knew exactly why I was there. My dad had done a number on me, I told Dr. Phil. (Truly, his first name was Phil, and I could not resist calling him "Dr. Phil.") I was thirty-two years old, and I already felt frayed at the edges. I was not an addict, an abuser, or a cheater. I was not anywhere close to a crisis point. Yet I felt I was living my life on shaky ground.

I told Dr. Phil that I worried I was capable of doing great harm to those I love. When I peered at the far horizon of my life, I wondered if I was destined, like my dad, to self-destruct before I made it.

How do I keep myself from following in his footsteps? How do I prevent myself from hurting my wife and kids?

At the time, the primary purpose of therapy as I understood it was to prevent you from damaging other people. Counseling was a tool you could use to generate better life results. I hadn't yet considered that I had healing to do for its own sake. I did not recognize just how much I was living in a story that was a continuation of the one that came before me and that I needed to read it carefully in order to keep writing my own.

But that's more or less where Dr. Phil began. He leaned back in his brown leather chair behind his worn secondhand desk. He listened as I explained that my main question was how to make sure I don't hurt those I love.

"Well," Dr. Phil said, "that's a good question. But why don't you start with a story?"

"Okay. About me? Or about my dad?"

"Let's go with your dad. Tell me a story about him."

I looked at the carpet and tried to figure out where to begin.

I could tell Dr. Phil about the night Mom got a call from the cops and sank to her knees in a scream of *No! No! No!*, one hand holding the lime-green receiver tight against her ear and the other gripping the phone's long, coiled cord like a line thrown from a passing boat. Dad, a traveling insurance salesperson at the time, had been arrested on drunk driving charges and was in some random jail in some random town, lucky he hadn't killed someone. I was maybe two or three years old and know of the night more through my sister's memory than my own, but in my mind's eye I can see Mom crumpled into our orange-brown shag carpet, against the backdrop of wood panels in our home in Jackson, Tennessee. I can see seven-or-eight-year-old Kaysie standing in her bedroom doorway, watching, then making her way over to Mom to put a comforting hand on her shoulder.

Or maybe I could talk about the time Dad took us on one of his road trips to Florida, where we planned to enjoy the beach and the sun and the water but where, instead, Dad installed us in a hotel room and then went drinking for uncountable hours, leaving his young family stranded without money, without food, without any way of knowing where he was or when he'd be back.

Then there are the many times random church people showed up to our front door with groceries, boxes of clothes, checks written out to Mom or Dad to help us get over one hump or another. I remember opening the door and seeing strangers smiling at me with cardboard boxes full of food. I remember small yellow envelopes with ten or twenty dollars inside, and how one time, one of them was given to me a couple of weeks before Christmas. I remember how I went to the smoke shop in the mall and bought Dad a pockmarked brown pipe for his stocking, thinking it'd help him kick the Kool Filter Kings habit.

I could talk about the time Dad lost his job in Huntsville, Alabama, and we promptly lost our apartment. But Dad had a backup plan, and then a backup to the backup. For over a year, Dad found us one short-stay arrangement after another, mostly thanks to Southern Baptists. Sometimes we had to help him win them over. I remember packed sanctuaries on Sunday mornings, Sunday evenings, Wednesday midweek services. Near the end of the services, we Dodds would go to the front and stand in a row—my dad, mom, sister, and me, dressed in secondhand Sunday best—and we'd look out at the pews of people. I remember hearing the pastor talk about what a precious family we were, how we were down on our luck, and how God called people like them to help people like us. I remember Mom and Dad crying in gratitude.

Skip forward a few years and a few more moves, and there's the time when I was fourteen and Dad caught me stealing one of his Kool Filter Kings. Actually, it was Mom who caught me, and it was almost midnight when she smelled the smoke coming from under the basement bathroom door. She went upstairs and woke up Dad. I heard the *boom boom boom* of him marching downstairs. I was still standing in the bathroom when he appeared in his thin blue bathrobe, a brown leather belt coiled like a snake in his right hand. "You're big enough to smoke?" he snapped. "You're not too big to be whipped!" He grabbed me by the arm, pulled me out of the bathroom, and pushed me into my room and then onto my bed. He proved his point across my back, my butt, my legs until it was all out of his system. It'd been many years since he'd whipped me, and he had some catching up to do.

The next day, after we'd exchanged apologies—me for stealing and for smoking, him for "going a bit too far"—I drew Dad a picture of a gravesite with a tombstone. The inscription read: "R.I.P./Smoking Kills." I was trying to show him I'd learned my lesson but also sending a sly warning about his own pack-a-day habit. At the time, I had not yet started fantasizing about his death.

I could tell Dr. Phil another story, from that same year, about the time Kaysie—five years older and away at college—was hospitalized with a severe depression that threatened her life. I remember that night as the first time I'd ever been able to access the anger that had been brewing in me for so long. I remember being clear in my mind about who was to blame for Kaysie's pain. I went downstairs to my room and imagined the walls were my dad. I punched them and kicked them until finally one of the walls gave way and I left a gaping hole right above the baseboard. Dad never mentioned the big gash, which stayed unpatched for the remaining years we lived in that house.

I could talk about getting my first job at the mall at fourteen years old and Dad asking me for some of my paycheck money and how I asked, "What do you need it for?"—knowing that the answer was, of course, booze. He took deep offense at the question and spent hours grinding me down until I could no longer remember why I ever, ever, *ever* questioned anything about him because he was always right and I was always wrong. I offered, in all sincerity, to just sign all my paychecks over to him going forward, and he said, "No, son, that isn't necessary. I just need you to know that when I'm asking for money, it's for a good reason." I felt grateful for his forbearance.

Then there are the stories I could tell about him not showing up—for anything, ever. Basketball camp, tennis matches, rugby games, whatever else I was doing. There's the morning of my high school graduation when Dad was too hungover to make an appearance. There's me standing on the football stadium field in my blue-and-green cap and gown, scanning the bleachers, and seeing only my mom and my sister. *I'm hungover, too, Dad*, I thought, *and I got here just fine.*

There's me finding his secret stashes of booze in the garage and dragging the bottles out so he'd know I knew. There's my freshman year of college when I was still living at home and things with Dad were really bad, about as bad as they had ever been. There's working up the courage to confront him about it—gathering all his hidden bottles from around the house and arranging them in a neat row on the kitchen table, then waiting for him to come home and forcing him to sit down and talk to me about it. There's him telling me—in a voice as stone cold sober as I'd ever heard—that he knew his drinking habits were a problem, but that he was under a lot of pressure. And if I wanted to know the source of that pressure, I could look in the mirror.

I asked him to clarify. "Wait, Dad, are you saying that I am the reason you drink?"

He looked to the side for a moment, trying to decide how he wanted to answer this question. Then he looked back at me. He gave me a cold, affirmative nod.

"Not just you," he added. "Your mom and sister too."

There's another time later in college when I was home for a visit and sitting up late, talking to Mom at the kitchen table. Dad should have been home hours ago, and we were talking about whether I should go looking for him when the door opened and he stumbled through it and spilled right onto the floor. I tried to help him stand, but he was too far gone. I picked up my father's pathetic, drunken ass and carried him to the upstairs bathtub, trying not to drop him while also fantasizing about a slip-and-fall that would make everything be over.

There's him showing up sauced to the rehearsal dinner for my sister's wedding. My sister and her friends were all teetotalers at the time, so I suppose Dad knew he'd have to pregame, and he'd been doing it all day.

There's driving him to Alcoholics Anonymous (AA) meetings in my early twenties and sitting in a circle with the other people in the program. There's hearing him say, "My name is Bill Dodd, and I'm an alcoholic." We'd sit and listen to the stories of people on their fifth, tenth, twentieth sobriety anniversaries. One time on the way home, I asked Dad if he ever thought he'd be one of those people with a lot of years of sobriety behind them. He turned to glare at me from the shotgun seat, then replied, "Not if you keep asking me about it."

There's in-patient rehab, and then rehab again, and then again.

There are the jobs he lost to drinking, and the drinking he did because he lost the jobs.

There's him calling me midmorning on a Saturday when I'm out running errands, his speech already slurred.

There's me telling him, finally, in my early thirties, that he wasn't allowed to call me ever again. Explaining that he wasn't allowed to come visit his daughter-in-law and his grandkids and me. That from now on, I was the one who would set the terms of our engagement.

There's him finding ways around my resistance and back into my life. There's me putting up walls I thought he could never scale, then watching him crawl his way up and over, a parasite of pathetic persistence.

Dad died when I was thirty-three, almost a year to the day after I started seeing Dr. Phil. Had I been able to peer into that near future, I could have answered Dr. Phil's question by telling him the story of Dad dying—drinking himself to death, basically, though he also had emphysema and melanoma and lung cancer and throat cancer and Lord knows what else.

Mom had finally left him months before, after four decades of praying that the Lord would make him a man. He spent his final months alone in his apartment with bottles hidden behind books and in drawers. Hidden from whom, exactly? My sister visited plenty, saintlike until the end, but most of the time it was just Dad and God in that apartment, the half-empty bottles tucked out of sight until we gathered them into trash bags a few days after he expired.

We didn't want to have a memorial service, but my sister's pastor told us we needed to see it through. We held Dad's funeral in an all-but-empty chapel in Tulsa—the only people there were my mom and my sister and I and our families. A few of my sister's friends came in solidarity. No one came to pay their respects to Dad, because who would?

So, okay, Dr. Phil. You want a story? Take your pick.

• • •

Finally, as I sat there looking at his carpet, Dr. Phil offered a suggestion.

"Look," he told me, "you don't need to dive in to the absolute best story you can think of. Actually, don't think about it at all, just, when I ask you to tell me a story about your dad, what is the very first one that comes to mind?"

I knew the answer to that question, but I did not want to admit it. What came to mind was a story I had never before told anyone—not because it was too dark, but because it wasn't dark enough. It felt inconsequential, unworthy of attention. All the same, it was a story I thought about all the time.

It was a story about a lawn mower.

3

The Lawn Mower

I'm five years old. My head abounds with sandy curls. My right hand clutches a knob of blue blanket. The blanket is raised to my face, where my thumb is lodged in my mouth like a breathing tube. Our glass kitchen door is my TV screen, and what's happening in the backyard is the show. My ten-year-old sister, Kaysie, is out there, a mite of freckles and jet-black hair, confident to the extreme—the person who should be in charge of things around here, so far as I can tell.

Kaysie is pushing a mower up and down our endless backyard. Endless not because we are owners of a large estate—endless because the lots did not need to be small, as people are not clamoring to live in this part of town. The neighborhood is a bramble of hills and homes tossed down at random by God.

Kaysie is barely taller than the mower handle, and I wonder how hard it is to push that machine. I wonder how soon I will be the one doing the pushing. My dad stands adjacent to her mowing, shirtless in summer's sauna. He keeps watch through a squint, smoking a cigarette and grin-grimacing under his amber-brown mustache. His jeans are cut off at mid-thigh. His bare chest is sunken, his belly round but taut, his wiry arms plugged into firm, round shoulders. Dad might look weak except for those upper arms. Plus his face, which is set like flint.

Suddenly, he waves those arms and cries out "NO! NO! NO!" until Kaysie cuts the engine.

Dad points up and down Kaysie's mowed rows, then back to the mower like a referee calling a foul. He kneels down to a two-inch mohawk row of grass that Kaysie has left in her wake. Kaysie looks at him blankly but nods. Dad is stern, and so is his daughter. He points at the missed grass again, flabbergasted. Then he reaches down and pulls the cord—Kaysie is definitely too small to do that—until the engine sighs out one dark cloud and sputters back to life. Then she is again pushing, him smoking and now smiling, like he's really accomplished something.

A quiet presence looms behind me. I look up to see that Mom is watching the same scene. She emits a small grunt.

That eternal lawn will not burden Kaysie's chore list for many more years, for soon Mom and Dad will lose the house and we'll embark on a sojourn of apartment complexes and borrowed homes where other people do the mowing. Finally, in the summer before my sixth-grade year, we move across the country to Colorado Springs and into a rental home with a sizable yard. The garage is stocked with a reel push mower, and Dad enjoys the novelty of the old-time machine. But not enough to use it himself. He points it out to me, says I'll probably need to go over the yard two or three times each weekend with that old thing. Each weekend, I do, and he inspects, and then I do it once more.

Before seventh grade, we move to a different Colorado Springs neighborhood. Dad has a new job, and Mom does, too, and they're able to get a loan and purchase a home. This one has a three-sided lawn—front and back plus a stretch running along the driveway. The previous owner had sodded the entire lawn with bluegrass and kept it watered and fertilized, and it is the thickest, greenest lawn any of us has ever seen. In celebration, my dad goes to Ace Hardware and buys an off-brand silver lawn mower. She is a beaut. He raves to Mom about what a good deal he'd found. He sings to himself in the garage as he screws on the wheels and fixes the mower handle and grass catcher in place.

And then it is time. Dad tells me to come watch. He starts her up and pushes up and down a couple of rows. He stops the engine to explain to me what he'd done, how he'd mowed straight and true in one direction, then circled back with four-to-six inches of overlap. That's how you avoid leaving mohawks of grass, he explains. He points out the neat lines left by the mower wheels in the grass, tell-tale signs of whether you've done the four-to-six-inch overlap. There's really no getting away with not doing it right, he says. The lawn tells the tale.

On this first Saturday of our new home, our joy is mutual. We take turns pushing our silver mower up and down. Our spines are as straight as our rows. The mower runs well and true, and when we are done, our lawn looks like the pitch at Wembley.

The next Saturday morning, it is time for my first solo flight. Dad shows me how to put gas in. He shows me how to start the engine. He acts like he is giving me a new car, and I very much feel that he is. *Son, I hereby bequeath to you this silver off-brand mower. She is a right fine machine.*

In my hands, she will not last for more than a couple of summers.

By the next year, mowing the lawn is no longer novel, but it remains my responsibility, along with trimming the edges and bagging all the clippings and setting the bags into a tidy queue on the side of the house and sweeping the garage with the push broom and then sweeping it again and maybe one more time, just to be sure. Friends would come over and see me sweeping, always sweeping, and say, "Wow, your dad is really serious about that garage floor."

One Saturday I get up and, after a bit of dillydallying—cereal with every word of *Sports Illustrated*, then a comic book or three—I go outside to get to work.

I check the gas tank, top it off, start up the mower, get moving.

About two-thirds of the way through the front lawn, the mower engine sputters to a halt.

Shit, I think. *What makes an engine stop?*

I've just put gas in, so that's not the issue. I don't know how to even begin to think about what might be wrong. I stand for a moment next to the dead mower. Dread sets in.

On Saturdays, I tended to wake up in hot water. Sometimes I barely had a chance to empty my bladder before I was in trouble for not yet mowing the lawn, and on this day, I'd already delayed the chore too long. Dad wanted me to bed down in the garage next to a shrine I'd made of our silver mower, counting the hours until I was blessed to pull her cord. And once the purring of the mower began, it better damn well continue, because everyone knows you check the gas before you pull the cord; otherwise, you're a fool, aren't you, Patton? Why would you start the mower before checking the gas? This mower engine has only so many pulls she can take over the course of her life, so what, you're going to start her with only a smidgen of gasoline? So then halfway through mowing, the engine dies? Now you're having to pull the cord a second time before you're even done with the front yard. You've effectively downgraded your lawn mower before getting even a side of the yard done, all because you were too lazy to check the gas level like everyone knows you're supposed to do.

I know Dad is inside, paying attention to the background noise of my mow, and my goal is to produce an engine purr that lasts as long as it should for the front, side, and backyards to be trimmed.

But for one reason or another, the mower has stopped. An uncut third of the front lawn is standing tall and glaring at me. Dad is somewhere in the house, surely noting the silence by now, knowing there's no way his lawn is finished. I look up to see if he's already walking out. Not yet—but wait, yes, his figure appears, standing in the living room window, watching me, waiting, wondering. Does he already know what's wrong with the mower? Does he know how to fix it? Does he think that I know how to fix it, and I am just standing here lazily because I am a lazy son? Or does he think I *should* know and am just standing stupidly because I am a stupid son?

    I kneel next to the mower, unscrew the gas cap, and confirm what I did not need to confirm: ample gas. I crane my neck this way and that, looking around the engine and all its parts, this doohickey and that, not knowing how any piece fits the whole or where to begin interrogating the thing. Dad remains in the window, watching me. I look more intensely. I try to look at the mower as if I know what I'm looking at, peering all around the engine like some kind of guy who knows how engines do what they do.

    Finally, I look up at the living room window and let Dad catch my eye. I shrug and shake my head.

    Dad opens the front door and lights a Kool Filter King, makes his way to me. "What's the problem?"

    "It just stopped. It's got plenty of gas. I refilled it before I started."

    He spins open the gas tank and peers inside. "It's got plenty of gas," he confirms. "Move over." He circles the mower, then reaches for the cord and gives it a couple of violent yanks.

I'm surprised at the power of his pulls—his wiry frame belies his strength.

The mower, alas, is unimpressed. It gargles and goes quiet.

"I think it needs oil," he says, definitively. "Go grab a bottle."

"Yes, sir," I say and head to the garage, hoping I know where the oil bottles are and what they look like. I find one, grab it, and head back out.

Dad has disappeared. The mower stands there, dead and alone.

I approach it and wait for him a moment or two.

Then I have a thought I will live to regret: *It just needs oil. How hard can this be?*

I kneel next to the mower and try to find a spout that says "PUT OIL HERE" or something like that. I look all around for a place that looks like an oil-getting place. Nothing leaps out.

I think on it for a moment. *Oil is a lubricant, and I bet it needs to work its way through the whole engine, so maybe the thing to do is pour it right on top, like chocolate syrup over a bowl of ice cream.*

I open the bottle and start to tilt it over the mower, then think better of it—*Wait, I've never seen an oil-soaked mower engine. I bet that's not the way.*

I smile to myself, relieved at the near miss. *Whew, close one, you idiot!*

I look at the gas cap again. Logic takes hold: *If on this engine there is only one place to put liquid things, and the engine needs oil, then I must put the oil in the place where you put liquid things.* The gas tank is the one place that looks like it takes liquid things. Ah! I've figured it out!

I spin open the gas cap. I tip the entire bottle of oil inside.

I give the oil a minute to settle, then stand to pull the cord. On the third or fourth yank, a dark cloud spins up and out of the mower like a ghost of death. The engine declares an awful whine, and the smoke doubles and triples—not a single ghost but a hundred ghosts, swirling all around the front yard. I am standing amid the spirits like an exorcised boy when Dad bursts across the lawn, waving his arms at me and yelling, "NO NO NO NO NO WHAT DID YOU DO OH MY GOD WHAT DID YOU DO?"

"I just put the oil in and tried to start it! You said it needed oil!"

"What do you mean you put the oil in?"

"I don't know! I just put it in, like you said."

Dad kneels next to the mower and spins open the oil cap. The oil cap! Ah, there it is! Somehow I'd missed the obvious.

Dad peers inside and then looks up at me.

"You put oil in here?"

I say nothing. I try to disappear before his very eyes.

"Patton, where did you put the oil?"

There's nothing to say. There is no way to say the words, "Dad, I put the oil in the gas tank." Those words would only confirm what he already knows: *Your son is an idiot.*

But he wants to hear it.

"Son, what did you do?"

"I put the oil in."

"*Where* did you put the oil?"

"I . . . I . . . I thought it went with the gas."

Dad bursts up from aside the mower and grabs me by the shoulders. He holds his face an inch from mine. He spits words. There's no fixing this, the mower is ruined, he cannot believe what I've done, goddammit, goddammit, goddammit.

I stand, frozen, to let him finish, not bothering to wipe my tears, but he cannot finish—his frustration has unspooled, and it just keeps coming. I have ruined his mower. I always make everything harder, make everything worse. I cannot be trusted to do the simplest little thing, and he's long suspected that I will ruin something valuable. And now I have. I have ruined his mower. His silver mower! Do I realize what I have done? Do I realize how much this will cost him? Do I realize how hard he works? How little he asks in return? Do I realize how many things I should know about being a man that I somehow still do not know? My stupidity is bottomless, unfathomable. There is no excuse for me.

Dad looks over at our front yard tree with its tiny branches. Is this a whipping offense? Will he make me choose a switch?

At some point, I crumple to the ground with hails of "I'm sorry! I'm so sorry!" I am prostrate before him and the mower. Dad looms over me, decides against whipping, storms away. I kneel in the grass and sob for a bit, then gather myself enough to sit cross-legged and wait to see if he'll return. He never does.

I walk to a neighbor's house and ask if they'll let me borrow their mower to finish our grass. They have a red one—a Honda, just like the car. It purrs nice and quiet, and when it needs gas, I add some and keep going.

• • •

We don't get to choose which memories hold weight. We can argue with ourselves about which memories should matter, but we'll lose those arguments—memories come at their own bidding. Even as I told Dr. Phil that story, I was questioning it from within. *Does any of this matter? Why are we starting here?* The only sure sign I had of its importance was how hard it was for me to tell it. I was sobbing like someone had just killed my dog.

Even so, half of me expected Dr. Phil to respond by saying, "You didn't know that you can't put oil in the gas tank?" The other half expected him to ask how I could be sure my dad was even drinking that morning. Can we verify that fact, please? Because this account doesn't have most of the features of your classic Alcoholic Dad story. No physical violence beyond a bit of shaking. He barely even curses. And anyway, I did ruin his mower. Any dad would get pretty frustrated with that.

Dr. Phil didn't say any of that. Mostly, he encouraged me to keep sitting with the story, to not let myself diminish it. He said we'd need to keep coming back to it, and we did, a little, even as we explored other stories. I could not afford to see Dr. Phil for very many sessions, but I did try to take his advice. I kept letting myself sit with the lawn mower story. I resurfaced it years later with another, longer-term therapist. I still was not sure why it was the story that always hung around the edges of my mind. I still felt like it was a nothing story, too inconsequential to share with anyone I wasn't paying to listen to me.

But it kept coming back to me. When I sat to write these very pages, I figured I'd draft it and discard it, put it to rest in a pile of deleted passages.

Instead, I finally found the source of its hold on me.

4

Missing the Obvious

HERE'S A STORY that my high school friends used to love to tell. It's the fall of 1991. It's my junior year, and I am partying in my friend Stacie's basement with a small group of pals. Four or five guys and four or five girls pounding red Solo cups of vodka and Kool-Aid and playing strip poker. (Note to any Dodd kids in the audience: Do as I say, not as I did.)

A few Solo cups into the game, I decide to pick up the pace of the stripping. I stand up and start dancing and singing along to the song that was pouring from Stacie's radio: Color Me Badd's "I Wanna Sex You Up." So now I'm singing and gyrating, slipping out of my shirt and then my pants, swinging them over my head and tossing them in the general direction of the girls. The girls are laughing, and the guys are laughing, and I am laughing.

But wait. Are they laughing *with* me or *at* me? Definitely *at* me, dummy. I am giving them an excess of reasons to laugh: the dancing plus the stripping plus the sing-shouting "Ah tick tock and you don't stop" plus—and here is the kicker—the bright white-and-red striped Mickey Mouse boxers I had donned that morning. I'm strutting around Stacie's basement with a waving Mickey on my fly.

All this is more or less good fun until the vodka makes its way back up the hatch and I begin puking all over everything and bringing the party to a full stop. Woe piles on top of woe, and before long I am crying to the whole room about what an awful alcoholic my father is and how I, picking drying puke from my chin, will never be anything like his drunk ass.

The story keeps going from there, as that night lasted forever and involved more people and more booze and more tears, then a near-disastrous episode of shit-faced me driving around a carful of people who took turns working the stick shift while I worked the pedals because I refused to let anyone else behind the wheel.

It's a funny-sad story, and as funny-sad is one of the best memoir tones, for a while I thought the story made for a good opener for this book. It has the nice irony of a drunken teenage boy crying about his dad's drinking. Hardy har har.

But for me, the story always had another layer, a prologue that was more embarrassing than anything else that happened that night: Until just a few days before Stacie's party, I did not even know that my father had a drinking problem. I had just figured things out, and I was pissed off at him. That is why I pushed the limits so hard that night. I was angry at the fresh revelation that my dad was a hopeless drunk.

This may not compute for you, I realize.

Given the many stories I listed above, the ones I flipped through while trying to give Dr. Phil a starter story, it may seem impossible that I did not know my dad was an addict until I was seventeen years old. He drank his way through fatherhood. How could I not have noticed? Well, I didn't. The truth is that in my experience of many of those stories of my childhood, a major plot point was missing. Until I was seventeen years old, I was Luke Skywalker living before the climactic light saber battle in *The Empire Strikes Back*, and I had no idea Darth Vader was my father. Everyone else knew— Leia, Obi-Wan, Han, even Chewbacca—but they kept little ol' Luke in the dark.

I knew that my dad had had a drinking problem when I was little. I can remember him driving us around with a can of Pabst Blue Ribbon in his hands. But I also believed that he'd been sober for many years. I don't know if I was ever even told that, but it's what I long believed. And then I found out I was wrong. Not just wrong, but oblivious. It was a crushing blow.

At Stacie's party, I told everyone I was getting wasted because my dad sucked at being a dad. That was half the truth, the half I could share without embarrassing myself. The other half, far more embarrassing than performing a striptease down to my Mickey Mouse boxers, was that I was getting wasted because I sucked at knowing things.

• • •

Earlier that week, I had gone for a walk in our neighborhood with my big sister. Kaysie had recently moved back home after being away at college for most of the previous four years. I'd basically been only-childing it since the seventh grade. Now, Kaysie was back and was going to be living with us for a while. I was so glad she was home.

She and I walked and talked about how things had been going at home. How weird and hard it had been. How things were always tense between Mom and Dad. How there was never any money for anything. It still always felt like we were going to lose our house again or not have groceries to get through the next week. Sometimes Mom would fret over how she was going to get back and forth to work each day since she did not have enough money to put gas in her car.

All this was life as we knew it and had always known it—I wasn't telling Kaysie anything unusual. Home was always full of hard. I was just sharing the latest hard.

At one point, I made a dumb joke: "I mean, things are so bad around here, Dad might as well start drinking."

Kaysie touched me on the shoulder and stopped me from taking another step. She turned and looked at me curiously.

"What do you mean, 'start drinking'?"

"I mean, you know, why not? He might as well be pounding booze. Like he used to, I mean. When we were little."

A pause hung in the air. Kaysie took a breath. "Patton, you know Dad is an alcoholic, right?"

"Um, sure, of course," I said. "Once an alcoholic, always an alcoholic."

"I'm not talking about when we were little kids," Kaysie said. "I mean now. I mean all the time. I mean our whole lives. Your whole life. He has always been drinking."

Another pause. I took it in.

"I thought he stopped."

"No. Maybe for a few months here and there, a couple times. But not for long. He's always been drinking."

Dad was right about me. I was the world's biggest idiot.

• • •

Dad never did his drinking out in the open—he had quit doing that sometime when I was a little boy. But he was not all that careful either. For the previous couple of years, during all those sweeps of our garage, I had been finding bottles of booze. Once I found a couple of massive glass jugs of cheap red wine sitting on a bottom shelf behind the buckets we used to wash the car. Another time I found bottles of vodka high on a shelf behind cans of spray paint. A third time, I'd discovered quarter pints of gin tucked behind a box of gloves.

Each time, my first thought was, *Oh crap, I hope Dad doesn't find this booze and think it's mine.*

I would pull the bottles out and bring them to Dad. Our conversations would go something like this:

"Hey Dad, check out these bottles I found."

"Oh, wow, son," he'd say. "Okay." He'd wait for me to say the next thing.

"I swear I've never seen these before."

"You haven't?" he'd say.

"No. I mean, I don't even know how they got there."

"You don't? That is . . . very odd."

"It is, I know. What do you think?"

"I don't know, son. This is . . . wow. This is not good. Better let me pour these out."

"Okay, Dad."

And then I would think, *Whew! Good thing he believes me.*

The booze bottles were a mystery, but I had a theory. My no-good friends—and I had my fair share of no-good friends—were stashing their booze in our garage. It made a kind of sense. We lived across the street from the middle school, and ever since seventh grade, local kids had used our backyard as a holding area for things they were not allowed to take to school (mainly skateboards, though one guy left some nunchucks and a switchblade one time). Another time, someone had stashed a dime bag of pot. Dad did not like these friends of mine, and he'd warned me that if they kept stashing stuff, he'd blame me, not them. But my no-good friends were cool and scary and I could never bring myself to tell them to stop putting their stuff in our yard.

When I found booze bottles, I reasoned that my cool/scary friends had gone from stashing stuff in our backyard to stashing stuff in our garage. Made sense to me. Until that walk with Kaysie, when I realized that my sense was nonsense.

Dad was not just right that I was an idiot—he was counting on it.

Dad's addiction was the most obvious, shaping fact of our family. Yet for years on end, it was lost on me. Yes, Dad could be volatile. Yes, he moved us around a lot. Yes, we lived on the knife-edge of poverty year in, year out. And sure, amid all this urgency, Dad spent a lot of time nodding off in the living room, his snores ripping the air like a jet turbine. But until I was seventeen years old, I was blind to the most basic element of our reality. I did not grasp the key feature of our lives. Mom knew, of course. Kaysie knew. Hell, *Dad* knew, even as he hid those bottles from us and God and even himself until his dying day. Our family back in Mississippi and Tennessee knew. Everyone knew.

Except me.

There was a reason we never had any money. There was a reason we had to stay in other people's homes and rely on local churches to bring us food. There was a reason my mom's mom and brother sent her twenty-five- and fifty-dollar checks so we could get a week's worth of groceries. We weren't just down on our luck. Dad was drinking harm and lack into our lives.

And I'd been oblivious to all of it.

I didn't understand how anything worked. I was always putting oil in the gas tank.

• • •

That was all thirty-plus years ago. And let me cut to the chase here: The degree to which I've moved on from my childhood is astonishing to me. I'm like, pretty good, you know? I'm not in the grip of any addictions. I'm treating people as well as I can. I have a great marriage to a woman I love. I love my kids and they love me back. My sister and I are still close. I have many good and admirable friends. I'm a reasonably mature, competent, and good-spirited person.

And yet. Childhood stories have a way of draping themselves over us. Or rising from within, all the time, unpredictably, in all sorts of ways.

In that story about the night at Alice's happy hour, when I burst into tears in front of a stranger, I said that I don't feel all that haunted by my upbringing. But the point of that story is that hauntings hide. If you're paying attention, you'll see signs of the spooking. Life can be a never-ending education in the reasons you are the way you are.

• • •

Typing sucks today because my right hand is wrapped in a bandage that cinches my pinky and ring finger together. The bandage wraps a cut—last night as my wife and I were cleaning the kitchen before bed, a fly was buzzing around, and I tried to kill it by clapping it between my hands. That's the best way to kill flies, IMHO, and I'm quite good at it. I once counted up my claps-to-kills ratio with my son over the course of a couple of weekends of cooking, and I was seven for ten. Solid!

Only last night's fly was sitting on the blade of an eight-inch chef's knife. I clapped it anyway, and so I also clapped the knife . . . and filleted my hand below my pinky.

I lurched toward the sink and flipped the faucet on.

"Did you kill the fly?" Michaela asked.

"Don't think so," I muttered, grimacing.

"Did you cut your hand?"

"Yep, pretty deep."

As Michaela helped me clean the cut and wrap my hand, she asked another question: "Did you notice the knife?" Fair question. But tricky to answer. *Of course I noticed the knife* is a stupid response, because if I'd noticed it, why did I proceed to clap my hands around it? *No, I didn't notice the knife* is also a stupid response, because, well, it's an eight-inch chef's knife, big and shiny and unmissable. Plus, as it happens, freshly sharpened by me that very morning.

I don't recall what I said next to Michaela, exactly, but once she'd bandaged my hand, we ended up on the couch having an ~~argument~~ complicated conversation about how hard it is to talk to me about Mindless Mistakes. And lo, my Mindless Mistakes are legion, plotted within a wide range of intensity. Wearing my shirts inside out. All. Day. Long. Wearing my *shorts* inside out with the pockets flapping at my side, which is admittedly next level. Forgetting a pan boiling on the stove until the water has evaporated to a scorch. Walking with my family downtown and leaving them a half block behind, lost in thought. Slamming my hip bone into the kitchen counter or a table corner. Slamming some other body part into some other hard, immovable object—and barely noticing that I've done it. On the regular, one of my kids will ask how I got the gross yellow-purple bruise that's on my arm or belly or thigh or lower back, and I will have no idea.

Then there's driving. Curbing my back tire when taking a corner too tight. Missing my interstate exit, forgetting that we have an actual destination and are not just driving aimlessly. In the past few weeks, I've had two work trips out of town, and on both drives to the airport I got a full exit past the San Antonio International Airport before remembering that I had a flight to catch. One night last fall, we were driving to a lodge in the Texas Hill Country and I passed my turn and didn't notice for many miles. Then Michaela and Lou *did* notice—"Weren't we supposed to go left back there?"—but I kept dismissing them—"No, this is the way! I've driven this a million times!"—until finally we ended up in a distant ranch town straight out of *Friday Night Lights*.

How did I handle their questions about how I'd missed the turn? About why I wouldn't listen to their input? Suffice it to say that I had some apologies to hand out later that night.

One story, famous in Family Dodd, is about the time I pulled out of a gas station and directly into a six-foot-deep ditch. Didn't brake, didn't pause at all, just tipped straight into it, my mind clearly somewhere other than behind the wheel.

"Did you see the ditch?" everyone in my family asked at once, from a forty-five-degree angle.

I could tell you similar stories that go all the way back to my high school days. My closest friends in those days called me "Slappy," a portmanteau of *sloppy* and *happy*. My buddy Matt coined it, his best attempt at describing a certain obliviousness that is just a part of who I am. He even made me a T-shirt to commemorate the nickname.

One of my college roommates, Carlos, used to do what he called his Patton Dodd impression. He'd pick up his car keys, put his finger through the key ring, flip them around and around, and walk through our apartment, saying, "Has anyone seen my keys?"

I've been lucky to have good-natured friends, and I'm luckier still to have a good-natured wife and kids. Their jibes are in jest. But they are hitting a spot that is more tender than they know: *Did you put oil in the gas tank?*

I like to think I'm pretty good at laughing at myself. But on this particular issue—Mindless Mistakes—my skin can be thin to the point of translucent. As the questions come, my calibrator breaks. I hear good-natured jibes as jabs: *Why do you suck so much?* Nothing anyone can say to me will land as they intend. I hear it all as accusation, and my response is to go into a crouch, absorb the blows. On my worst days, I punch back. Even when I don't lash out at others, I lash at myself, deep within. You should see the marks I make.

I've never quite understood why I respond the way I do. I don't *want* to be so defensive about these silly Mindless Mistakes. They are, in fact, funny. Why am I so touchy?

Being absent-minded is not the same thing as being ignorant or unaware. But in my experience, they're close cousins. My persistent, self-accusing fear has long been that everyone else sees things I do not see. Everyone else knows oil doesn't go in a gas tank. Everyone else can tell that their couch-sleeping father is not just tired; he's an everyday drunk.

Adult life gives this insecurity a sharper edge because adult life is full of rudimentary tasks that take some know-how. Adult males arguably feel this pressure to an extreme degree because our cultural ideals of what a man is—and what a father is—emphasize *competence* across a range of tasks. I've spent my adult male life twisted into knots about my basic chops and lack thereof. How do you do anything that needs to be done? Buy a car? Operate that car? Deal with its various dashboard lights and weird sounds and drips on the driveway? How do you create a budget? Shop at the grocery store for a family of two, three, four, five? How do you hang a mirror? Fix a sink? Repair a fence? That broken lamp—do you just throw it away? Is it the kind of thing that is fixable? How do you vote? How do you figure out who to vote for? Can you really know? How do you do your taxes? Where do you file things? What do you do if you throw away things that need to be filed?

Then there is work. How do you run a meeting? Create a proper spreadsheet? Deliver on the deliverables that everyone is talking about in this meeting? Do they all understand what we're talking about? Are you the only one who is lost here?

Then there is religion. How do you believe in God? How do you understand anything in the Bible? How do you go to church and go along with the creeds and the songs and the prayers and the general all-encompassing culture of "Yes, this is totally what I think, too"? You're the adult—heck, you're the *man*—and you're supposed to be the one leading your family in the matter of faith, or so you've been told. But how?

Everyone else gets these things. Why don't I?

Where was all this competence supposed to come from? My dad, I suppose? What am I supposed to do if he didn't deliver?

I recognize that we're all filled with ignorance. What I'm listing here are feelings more than actual questions. We all have lots to learn, with varying degrees of confidence about what we know. We all need each other to fill in our gaps. But I find that I (like you, yes?) live most of my days believing that everyone else is Neo in *The Matrix* and they have downloaded all the requisite information and skill sets. Understanding and knowledge comes easy to them. It comes hard to me.

I could not have explained all this to you even a few months ago. I could have told you the lawn mower story, and I could have told you that I'm an absent-minded guy. But until recently, I had never connected the two things. It seems pretty obvious as I'm laying it out here, but the truth is that it took writing this very book for me to put these things together. It took storying myself. Now I can name something I've never before been able to name, which is that my deepest fear is that

I am a fool. I've carried that fear for as long as I can remember, in every season and context of life—presentations at work, discussions with my family, dinner parties with friends, debates even on topics that I know backward and forward. I'm a ball of insecurity, bracing for the next time I'm exposed as an ignorant ass.

I feel this fear even as I have learned to do many of the things that used to handicap me. Today, in my late forties, I am a reasonably competent man. I manage our budget okay. I'm a decent cook, and I keep my knives sharp and pans cleaned and oiled. I've fixed some things on our cars. I've hung mirrors, repaired leaky faucets, installed toilets. I learned to do these things gradually. Painstakingly. Lotta reading. Lotta asking for favors. Lotta YouTube. But I have learned them.

Which—I am telling you this so that I will tell myself—is another clue to who I really am. I'm not the kid who put oil in the gas tank. I'm the man who puts oil in the—what's it called? An oil tank? I dunno, but I do know what goes where. I'm a learner, not an accident-prone fool. Accident-prone, sure, and absent-minded. But those are just adjectives, not nouns. My Mindless Mistakes are not revelations of who I really am. Frustrating as hell but not determinative.

Recurring memories can be clues about the parts of ourselves we need to pay attention to. That's what the lawn mower story was for me, and I now see its nagging presence in my head as a gift. It was an origin story but not for all of who I am. It was just the story of a part of me that needed tending.

• • •

Which brings me back to my father.

I've long wondered what he would have gained from telling his own story—and what we would have gained. He never would do it, not even close. He hid his bottles; he hid himself. But what if he'd answered our questions about his childhood? What if he'd gone to a therapist or even a pastor and, you know, really talked? What if he'd made actual friends and shared his story with them?

No one came to Dad's funeral, not because they were rejecting him but because hardly anyone knew him enough to care that he'd died or that he'd lived. I think that was his dying wish—for no one to know who he was. But that's not what he should have wanted. It wasn't good for him, and it wasn't good for us. I do not want to grant it to him.

Which is how I ended up driving across the Deep South in late April 2023, from Florida to Mississippi to Alabama to Tennessee. It's how I ended up sitting in that graveyard in Louisville, on my dad's unmarked spot, then tracking down Dad's old drinking buddy, David Wilson. It's how I got to hear David say the last thing I could have ever expected anyone to say: "Billy Dodd is a legend in this town."

Thanks to that trip, it'll no longer be true that I don't know who my dad was. It'll no longer be the case that he's escaped me. Over the course of a few days in April 2023, I learned more than I'd known in the previous four-plus decades of life. Not everything, but enough. After a lifetime of not having much of a clue about my father, I have come to know why he was the way he was. I have come to know the legend of Bill Dodd.

5

The Legend of Bill Dodd

IN THAT FIRST phone call with David Wilson, he agreed to spend the next day with me. We met on a bench outside the courthouse and dove right into conversation. David and my dad had both grown up in Louisville, Mississippi, a town of about five thousand people in the last mid-century. Everyone knew everyone, but David says he didn't really get to know my dad much until their college years, when Bill Dodd became known as "Toddy Doddy," which is what David and other locals call him to this day.

Toddy Doddy was a popular sort, said David, "always had pretty girls on his arm," and he was even elected head cheerleader at Mississippi State University (MSU). While Dad attended MSU, David went to the University of Mississippi (Ole Miss), but they were both members of the Pi Kappa Alpha fraternity. Every couple of months, the two fraternity chapters would join forces to throw a major party at one of their houses. All you could drink and more, and they'd bring in bands, "big bands from New Orleans," said David, and even national acts on occasion. "We'd have the stars come in."

That reminded me of the one story Dad had ever told my sister and me about his time in college—that he'd once partied with Johnny Cash. Dad told us that Johnny had even left behind one of his famous jackets, later lost in a fire when the frat house burned down. We never knew if any of it was true, but now I finally had someone to ask.

"Did y'all have Johnny Cash come to the frat house one time?"

"Oh yes," David said brightly. "He and Johnny got put in jail."

"*What?*" This was news. "My dad and Johnny Cash?!?!"

"Oh yes," David said. "I came down for the concert, had a great concert in Starkville on campus. Then Johnny came over to the fraternity house with some of my friends, and they all got drunk. And then Toddy Doddy and Johnny were walking downtown, on the sidewalk, about three o'clock in the morning, and Johnny walked into a lady's yard and picked some flowers. The cops saw 'em and arrested 'em and put 'em in jail."

Johnny Cash fans know a version of this story. The song "Starkville City Jail" on the *At San Quentin* album (1969) is Cash's account of the time he was arrested "for picking flowers." Cash's version leaves out the Pi Kappa Alpha house party along with the actual reasons he was arrested—public drunkenness, trespassing, and indecent exposure. His version also has no mention of Toddy Doddy, and neither does any other historical record. After talking to David, I spent a few weeks calling sheriff's offices, circuit courts, chancery clerks, and the friendly folks at the Mississippi Department of Archives and History. I found a lot of well-meaning Southerners who did their best due diligence at my behest but no confirmation that Bill Dodd was ever booked with Johnny Cash.

But I did finally find one clue to Dad's presence. In May 2021, the Mississippi Country Music Trail Commission placed a historical marker near the jailhouse in Starkville, commemorating the event. I found a local news story online about the installation of the marker, complete with an image of it. Zooming in on that marker, I saw a photo. Zooming in on that photo, I saw twenty-three-year-old Bill Dodd, my future father, hamming it up with Johnny Cash and a bunch of his frat brothers.

Photo courtesy of Pi Kappa Alpha Fraternity. All rights reserved.

When I first saw that photo, I felt like the camera's eye in the last shot of *The Shining*, pulling in closer and closer to reveal that, yes, *he was there all along*. Of course, I already knew he'd been at the party. But he'd also been *there*, a person doing things in the world. Bill Dodd in a crowd of friends. Bill Dodd a few feet away from one of the greatest American artists of all time, kicking back whiskey and beer. Bill Dodd knowing people and being known, having a nickname. Bill Dodd, a young man in full, up and out in the world. He hadn't yet descended completely into himself, to that place where no one could find him.

• • •

For most locals in Louisville, the legend of Bill Dodd begins and ends there, more or less. But for David, the night with Johnny Cash was just one of many epic nights with Toddy Doddy.

David couldn't remember when my dad left the area. He didn't know that Toddy Doddy had never graduated, didn't know what he did for a living. At some point, Toddy Doddy was just gone. But in the years after David finished school and settled back in Louisville to start his law practice, Toddy Doddy started coming back.

"He wouldn't tell me he was coming," said David. "I'd just hear him pull up and then a knock on the door. And I knew what was going to happen." They'd catch up for a few minutes, then Dad would say, "Let's go get a drink." They'd hit the road with a bottle of whiskey and let the night become what it wanted to be. That was the pattern. David was living his life—practicing law in central Mississippi, dating beautiful women, never marrying or having kids. For years on end, Toddy Doddy would occasionally show up unannounced at David's door and join his life for a night.

I wondered how many years on end we were talking about. And when were these years? Right after college? Or was this into Dad's married-with-family years? Had Dad ever mentioned getting married? David couldn't recall. Having kids? David didn't think so. "We never talked about anything serious," David said.

David and I drove around Louisville and spoke for hours. Late in the day, David showed me where he lived in the years when Toddy Doddy was coming for visits. We sat in his old driveway, looking at the front door.

"I can visualize him pulling out of the driveway drunk, and turning and going in that direction," he said, pointing down the street.

"What years did you live in this place?" I asked him.

"It was a long time," he said. "Musta been . . . 1973 . . . up until about 1990."

I was born in 1974. And as we sat in David's car, I knew for the first time what Dad was up to in some of our hardest years as a family. I knew what he was doing on all those long road trips he took to sell insurance when I was a kid. I knew what he was doing while Mom was back home, counting on someone from church to bring us a bag of groceries. I knew what he was doing while Mom was on her knees, praying every morning and night that God would save her husband and family. I knew what he was doing after writing "Lord, Make Me a Man."

David was still processing the timeline. "I just don't . . . I know that must be right." He looked at me. "What year did he marry your mother?"

"1968."

He looked out his windshield, a realization dawning about his nights with Toddy Doddy.

"So all that happened *after he was married*?"

• • •

It was time for me to get on the road. David drove me back to where I'd parked that morning. He put his car in park and let it idle. He turned to me, grabbed my hand, and squeezed it. "I can't defend him," he said, looking me in the eye. "But he was a good friend, and I loved him."

"I hear you, David. Thanks for telling me that."

"You have to be *elected* head cheerleader, you know," he told me. "You can't be that unless people like you, admire you. Alcohol got ahold of him, but . . . you do have something to be proud of."

He was offering a tender point, and I did not argue it, even as it was hard for me to imagine the person David was talking about. The legend of Bill Dodd is that he was Toddy

Doddy. I never knew Toddy—I had seen only bare glimpses, perhaps when the blood-alcohol level was just right, of the gregarious, fun-loving man who loved being around people and whom people loved being around. That is who Bill Dodd was for a few years in central Mississippi. But it's not the father I got.

A few days later, I finally understood why.

• • •

I spent the next couple of nights in my mom's world—northern Mississippi and Alabama—having dinner first with her three surviving siblings and then with her second husband and some of his family. Their stories and insights are sprinkled throughout the pages of this book—I could footnote facts and observations throughout to Aunt Karen, Uncle Mike, and Aunt Beth, who regaled me with their experience of watching their cherished sister rush into marriage with a man none of them had ever heard of.

But the true north of my wayfinding on this trip was Jackson, Tennessee. I was going to have a sit-down with my father's older sister, Mabel, a woman I grew up calling Me-Me.

I adored Me-Me when I was a child. She and Uncle Bobby had us over all the time in the years we lived in Jackson, and their home was a haven. I thought Me-Me and Bobby were rich. They were nothing of the sort—like my parents, they'd started off in a low-income housing complex called Westwood Gardens—but their place brimmed with fresh sweet tea and just-caught trout and a freezer full of elk and deer and homemade banana ice cream. Glass dishes with mints or chocolate sat on end tables. The kitchen counter held bananas and oranges and baked goods from Me-Me's oven.

Sometimes Kaysie and I got to spend the night, and those nights were my favorite because on top of Me-Me's fridge were tall Tupperware containers of Cheerios and Frosted Flakes and Lucky Charms. Me-Me would let me have all the bowls of cereal I could handle.

When my dad moved us away from the South when I was little, he moved us away for good. I'd seen Me-Me and Bobby maybe three times since my early childhood. Bobby passed away not long ago, but Me-Me was by all accounts doing quite well—able and active at ninety.

When I first decided to write this book, I assumed a conversation with Me-Me was the place to begin. I started reaching out through my cousin Beverly to arrange a conversation. But it was tough to arrange. Me-Me was reluctant to talk, and she resisted politely but persistently. I eventually had it confirmed through another family member that she didn't want to talk to me about her brother. Kaysie had visited Me-Me a few years before and they'd had a long conversation about Dad, and apparently Me-Me never wanted to do anything like that again. The subject was more painful to her than we had known.

After a year or so, I let Beverly know I would be coming to Jackson to do research on my father one way or another.

How about we at least get together to catch up? She agreed to arrange an evening for us—her, Me-Me, Cousin Kenny, BJ (Kenny's wife), and me. We met up in an old downtown Jackson diner where they seemed to know everyone who walked through the door. We kept the conversation light. We went back to Beverly's place for brownies and more convivial conversation. I watched throughout the evening as kids and grandkids from across this family texted and called and FaceTimed. Beverly, Kenny, and BJ were play-by-playing everyone's lives for Me-Me's delight.

They were just as I remembered them: tight-knit, fun-loving, *together*. Whenever we visited Me-Me's house when I was little, it felt like a family reunion: moms and dads, kids, grandkids, nieces and nephews, cousins. Me-Me was nine years older than Dad and had gotten married at sixteen. She'd started a family early, and that family had both grown up and coalesced around her. They had their own nickname for her—everyone on that side of the family knows her as NoNo. Me-Me/NoNo's family went to church together, had dinners together, vacationed together, worked together, knew each other's stories by heart, finished each other's sentences. No one ventured very far from home, at least not for long. The contrast with her brother's family could not have been starker.

I loved being in their mix, and all evening long I was torn between enjoying our night and interrupting the flow with questions no one wanted me to ask. But finally, I took a leap. I told them that we needed to talk about why I had come to town. I told them about my book project. I told Me-Me that I knew nothing about her and Dad's family, and if she didn't want to provide information, I would understand. But I had just one question for her.

"You and Dad came from the same home, but you've built completely different lives. The family cultures the two of you created are worlds apart. Why do you think that is?"

The whole room froze for a moment.

Me-Me sat up straight in her chair and looked into my eyes. Then she gave me a great and costly gift: she answered the question.

"My mother created him," she said. "I don't know how to explain that boy, but she molded him from the time he was born."

"Molded him into what?"

"Into what she wanted. Billy was her god," she said. She said the relationship between mother and son shaped the whole home—who could eat what, who slept where, how money was spent. What about his relationship with his dad? "Zero," said Me-Me. Family life was dominated by a mother-and-son dynamic Me-Me described as obsessive. "She thought he was the only thing that existed."

Big Mama lived with us for a few years when I was little, and Dad could hardly stand being in the same room as her. He avoided her like the plague even when we were crammed into a small apartment. I always thought he was a jerk to his mom. I mentioned this to Me-Me.

"Well, you know why," she said.

"No, why was that?"

"Because of the relationship she had with him."

"Was it perverted?" I asked. Several seconds of silence ticked by.

"Well, they slept together," she said. For his entire childhood. When little Billy was born, his mom moved him into her room and into her bed. She kicked her husband out—for good. Billy stayed in his mom's bed throughout his entire childhood, up until he was fifteen or sixteen years old.

"Billy was who she loved," Me-Me said. "Twisted love."

My cousins and I sat and listened with dropped jaws. We asked follow-up questions, and Me-Me answered those too. She told us about how he started drinking as a kid, becoming a regular drunk by fourteen or fifteen. She told us family secrets that will remain family secrets not to be revealed here. She told us she'd spent her life working to forget the stories she was telling us. "I have tried to bury all that back in my mind," she said.

After a while, she asked if we could stop talking. She was starting to remember more, and she wanted some things to stay forgotten.

But Me-Me also told me something else. About halfway into our conversation, she paused and looked at me. "Patton, you are loved," she said.

"Thank you, Me-Me," I said.

A little later, she caught my eye and said it a second time. "Patton, you are loved."

As we hugged goodbye at the end of the night, she said it a third time. "Patton, you are loved."

"Thank you, Me-Me," I said. "I know I am."

And I did know. I do know. Her stories were a sacrifice of love.

• • •

Throughout the evening with Me-Me, I kept thinking about something a priest pal of mine often says: "Anything true can be talked about. Anything that can be talked about can be talked about well." That's a call to bravery: We can say the things that need to be said, and we can say them with care. The troubles that live inside us maintain their power by staying unspoken and unstoried.

• • •

I stayed with Beverly that night, and we sat up until the wee hours processing everything and sharing more stories from our lives. As I got on the road the next morning, I was alone with my thoughts and four or five hours of windshield time. Until then, I'd barely had time to process anything I'd learned in recent days, including the revelations about the kinds of things Dad was up to when Kaysie and I were little and Mom was going it alone. Those stories had given me fresh anger toward my father.

But I had to admit that I was feeling something else for my father, something new. I felt compassion.

I've met my fair share of guys like Bill Dodd in my life, guys who have made a mess of their lives in the wake of twisted upbringings. You meet people like this in churches. You meet them as a reporter. You meet them as you build a broad community of friends, especially if you have a somewhat twisted upbringing of your own. I've come across a lot of Bill Dodds in this world full of woe.

Each time I meet people like this and hear their stories, my reflexive response is the same: *I get it.* You've made jack shit of your life so far? You drink too much? You have a hard time holding down a job? You manipulate people? Well, what else would you expect, given what you come from? How could you possibly have become a solid, upstanding citizen? How could you possibly know how to love? I want all those things for you, and I want you to want those things, but it's easy to see why you've not been better formed.

The name for that reflex is *compassion*. That is exactly what I would have had for Bill Dodd if I had encountered him as a stranger.

Yet my dad was no stranger. He wrote "Lord, Make Me a Man," then unmade his manhood every day. All my life, he chose booze over us. He drove us into debt and desperation. He cut off all our family ties. He cut off all his friends and refused to make new ones. He could have made different choices. He had all he needed to guide him to health. He had AA. He had in-patient rehab. He had Kaysie and me. He had a wife who gave him forty years' worth of second chances. He pissed it all away.

Yet Billy Dodd was an abused boy for all the years of his raising. "My mother molded him," said Me-Me, and I now carry images in my head of that molding. "Lord Make Me a Man" might have been sentimental hogwash, but it was also a prayer of desperation. It was a manual for creating his own manhood from scratch, because none had been given to him. Could he have gotten there? Found stability? Chosen sobriety? Sure he could have, because miracles happen. But the deck is stacked against miracles.

For the rest of my life, thanks to Me-Me, I get to hold these truths about my father in tension. I will always count that tension as a gift. It's much better than things being tilted in one direction. Tension is a strain, but it's also the force by which we find and maintain balance.

It's been a year and a half since I talked to Me-Me, and I've noticed a difference in my chest when my dad comes to mind. I will always grieve the pain and suffering he caused, especially for my mom and sister. I will lament what needs lamenting. But I also find myself wishing for something new. I imagine a different Bill Dodd, one who discovered that anything true can be talked about. I imagine him finding a confidant, finding the courage and strength to tell his story. I imagine my father being free.

Part 2

THE ONES YOU MAKE

We are formed by little scraps of wisdom.

—Umberto Eco

6

Papa Friend

COMING FROM A guy with serious dad issues, this is going to sound a bit on the nose, but when I was a little boy, my imaginary friend was named Papa Friend.

I played with Papa Friend all the time, and I talked about him too. Mom would often ask how Papa Friend was doing. I saw him clear as day: short, trim, sporting a shaggy salt-and-pepper beard. He had two outfits, one of blue overalls and one of a brown baggy corduroy suit. The years had weathered Papa Friend's face, and he hunched his shoulders as he walked beside me with his knobby wooden cane.

But Papa Friend was spry, and he was game. He could do all the things I could do. We wrestled in the backyard and he let me win every time. We climbed neighborhood trees, perched ourselves on branches, and peered at my sister playing with her real friends below. We sat together on a chair in the living room and looked through the same books over and over.

In the years I palled around with Papa Friend, my family lived in Jackson, Tennessee. Occasionally, we'd drive two hours to Belmont, Mississippi, a tiny town where my mom had grown up and her mother and some of her extended family still lived. There's not much to look at on the highway between Jackson and Belmont—not much in the 1980s and still not much today. I'd stare out the window and imagine Papa Friend and I riding our bikes through the open fields that ran along the roadside. We rode like video game characters, bunny-hopping tall signs, popping wheelies on the rails of train tracks. Approaching overpasses, we'd speed up the exit ramps, launch giant double backflips, and stick the landings on the other side.

Every now and then, our family car would pass a ramshackle barn or crumbling clapboard home. I'd call out from the back seat, "That's Papa Friend's house."

"That one right there?" Mom would ask, pointing.

"Yes, that one right there," I'd say. I'd talk about how he was fixing it up and I was going to help.

Sometimes on those family road trips, I did not play with Papa Friend because my big sister would build another world for me to hang out in. She'd take my blue blanket or one of our grandmother's knit quilts and tuck its edges under the headrests in front of us, stretch them over the back seat, and use books and pillows to pin them down toward the rear window. We'd live under the canopy for hours. Dad's menthol smoke would waft back, a signal from another tribe.

Sometimes Kaysie didn't want to make a canopy world, didn't feel like talking at all. Sometimes the whole car was quiet. In those empty spaces, I would forget for a while that I had Papa Friend. I'd sit and not know how to fill the blanks in my head. The minutes would pass like days.

Finally, Mom would offer an assist from the front seat. "Patton, is that Papa Friend's house?" She'd point out whatever sorry shack we happened to be passing.

"Yes, that's Papa Friend's house," I'd say. And then I'd remember that I had something to do, someone to play with, someone who was there, always there, if only I would remember to summon him.

• • •

To paraphrase Voltaire's famous saying about God, if fathers did not exist, it would be necessary to invent them. And if the fathers who do exist do not father us—if our dads don't dad—we might make someone who will. That's what I was doing with Papa Friend. He was not just an imaginary being. He was a prototype, a first model of the many father figures I would go on to create.

All my life, I have been a maker of father figures. I've met men at church and school and work, friends of friends, guys who attend the same professional conferences. I've admired them, felt drawn to them. I've wanted them in my life. I've struck up friendships that became mentorships that have a chance to become something deeper—a relationship with a man who could be there, always there.

We don't tend to think of father figures this way, as things we make. We tend to think of them as things that already exist in the world. They are archetypes created by artists—King Lear, Atticus Finch, Marlin the clownfish. They are images in our life's landscape—coaches, teachers, bosses, elders. Father figures don't have to recognize us or even know us. They are publicly available representations of ideal dads. We obtain their benefit from afar.

But in my experience, father figures are also an active pursuit. They are a noun that is also a verb: You *father figure* people, collecting the wisdom and ways of being that your child self still needs. Do you do it on purpose? Are you even aware? Not necessarily. Father figures can be made by a reflexive act of our hearts, as involuntary as a yawn. Before we know we've done it, we've shaped our images of the people we know into the dads we need them to be.

When you father figure someone you know, you hope it's reciprocal—that this guy will see the child in you just as you see the dad in him. Some of the men I'll mention in what follows surely saw themselves as mentors, ministers, big-brother types who were down to teach me a thing or two. But for me, they were *more*. In my imaginative heart, I figured them as father and me as child, wishing to be raised in the way I should go. A wandering pilgrim, I wanted to be led, but I also wanted to be nurtured. I wanted to be known in the way a father knows his child.

It has taken me an embarrassing number of hours to summon up the nerve to write the last few paragraphs. Putting this out there feels risky. Sure, young boys and men looking up to older men is the most normal thing in the world. But that doesn't make it easy to talk about the longing. I take pride in being transparent with my closest friends, but very few of them have ever heard the story of Papa Friend. I don't talk about my lifelong, profligate father-figuring.

But I'm shaking off the sense of shame, because shame doesn't tell us the truth. There is nothing wrong—or even weird—about trying to fill our dad-sized gaps. We can hardly do otherwise. We are baby sea turtles making our way to the water. We don't know why we're doing it. We're just *being*, and being requires certain things of us. One thing being requires is fathering.

I mean this in the least patriarchal way possible.

The evolutionary anthropologist Anna Machin of Oxford University argues that the phenomenon of fathering as we know it is rooted in our very DNA. In *The Life of Dad: The Making of the Modern Father* (Simon & Schuster, 2018), she lays out a story of human fatherhood that begins over five hundred thousand years ago, well before *Homo sapiens* even existed. One of our ape ancestors, the *Homo heidelbergensis*, became the first primate to feature what Machin calls "investing fathers"—dads who stuck around. Most male primates, she jokes, screw and flew, like in most other species. But males in *Homo heidelbergensis* families got involved in the care and feeding of their offspring.

Why did this happen? Evolutionarily speaking, it had to—the survival of the species depended on it. Babies like us are born, says Machin, with "the helplessness of a puppy but the open eyes and ears of a chimp." We're a lot to handle—"dependent, immobile, energy-hungry." If babies like this were going to survive against the odds, primate moms needed primate dads to stay close and do things for the kids—make and control fire, hunt for high-protein sources of food, co-operate with others . . . and teach their kids to do the same.

Machin's research also shows that fatherhood is about more than mere survival. It's about flourishing. Multiple studies indicate that the extended presence of fathers is associated with all sorts of positive outcomes. Infants breastfeed better and gain weight more regularly when fathers are around. With invested dads, babies are more likely to form proper emotional bonds. Then, they're more likely to pursue advanced education, find stable jobs, and experience mental wellness.

It can be hard to talk about these things without sounding like a family values scold. Fatherless families and bad-father families are as common as can be. The United States—ground zero of family values sloganeering—has more single-parent households than any country in the world. Here, one in four children are growing up in a one-parent household, the vast majority of which—80 percent—are led by mothers. Those numbers do not even include families like the one I grew up in, where the dad is home but might as well be gone—too addicted, addled, or otherwise checked out to do any decent fathering.

Families can rise above all kinds of fatherlessness in all kinds of ways. Mothers can be more than strong enough to do the raising, should they have to go it alone. Mine was, and you'll soon see her strength overtake these pages, just as it overtook my life. Her mom was more than strong enough too—Mom's dad died when she was five years old, leaving behind a young wife with four kids ages six and under. She had to go it alone too.

Other relatives may also step up to do the raising—grandparents, aunts and uncles, even siblings take up fathering slack. My sister sure did. Born five years before me, Kaysie had it worse than I did, as firstborns often do in dysfunctional families. But for her brother's sake, Kaysie met the challenge of her ass of a dad. Dad would start to teach me something but lack the patience or sobriety to stick it out. Kaysie kept coming up from behind to finish the job. She was the one who taught me to climb those trees I got into with Papa Friend. She was the one who taught me to ride a bicycle. All my childhood memories of wrestling and tug-of-warring and tossing around balls are with her. She taught me to read. She taught me to write by hand. When I turned fifteen, she was the one who got me behind the wheel of a car. Later, she taught me to drive a stick.

With a sister like that, who needs a dad?

Apparently, we all do. I've tried—lordy, I've tried—to deny it. For years, I whistled my way through the father void in my life. But it's high time I admit that there's no ignoring it. Like it or not, the loss, absence, or negligence of a father cannot help but leave an impact. It is a wound that nature will try to heal. And by "nature," I mean *our* nature, our own raw material.

If we haven't had proper fathering, we're going to go looking for it. We're going to seek repair. And we can repair—fatherlessness is not an injury that puts us out of commission. It's just a wound we have to treat.

We have to make some Papa Friends.

7

Lord, Make Me Some Men

I'D LIKE TO throw a dinner party for all the men who have been father figures to me. The table would have to be long, the mood generous. They may not all like each other. I've been promiscuous in my father figure pickups, collecting them across a gamut of life experiences. I've taken on, at various times and to varying degrees, their politics, their postures, their approaches to life's big commitments—family, money, God. My father-figure dinner party would be a realized culmination of the conversation these guys have been having in my head for years.

I've gone with them to rock shows, Broadway shows, midnight drag shows. I've gambled with them in Vegas. I've snowboarded alongside them and run with them up and down long alpine trails. I've met them for coffees. I've met them for cocktails. I've joined their book clubs. I've sat with them in bars, sipping beers until we closed the place down, getting a good bit merrier than we planned but also going deeper into our truths than we would have otherwise. I've met them for hangover brunches the next day, stoking the embers of our conversations.

I've joined their Bible studies and prayer groups. I've spoken with them in tongues of angels. I've recited their old-school liturgies. I've raised my hands in the air and danced in worship with them. I've genuflected next to them at altars. I've felt them place Communion wafers on my tongue. The first time I met a priest, he took me to breakfast after a weekday morning Eucharist. I asked if I should call him Father.

"Oh, no pressure to do that," he said.

"I was kinda hoping I could," I said.

I've had them teach me to build wooden fences, mix and pour concrete, clear trees, install toilets. I've borrowed sizable sums of money from them. I've clocked their interactions with their wives and children. I've studied under them to get advanced degrees. I've written their names on the dedication page of my first published book; I couldn't choose just one ("To Ted, Kyle, and Michael . . ."). I've pitched them articles we might write together and syllabi we might teach together. A few times, they've pitched *me*, and *OMG*.

I cannot claim to have put all this father-figuring to the best possible use. It's just part of what I've spent my life doing—trying to fill in the gaps my dad left, and the gaps he can't even be blamed for. I didn't always know I was doing it. It's only upon reflection that I can see how much I've craved influence in every season of my life, not the kind you spread but the kind you absorb.

• • •

Father-figure-seeking can be instinctual and unconscious, but for a time in my youth, my search became deliberate. I remember the day it began.

"Patton, you need a man in your life," my mom said to me one morning. "I've been asking God to send you one."

We were on the phone on a midwinter Saturday, me in Fort Collins, Colorado, and her two hours south at our home in Colorado Springs. I was twenty-one years old, and I was flailing: lonely, broke, mired in doubt and dread. I was enrolled at Colorado State University (CSU), my third college in my third town in three years. I was seriously considering transferring again.

In keeping with my raising, I was moving around a lot.

At nineteen, for my first year of college, I'd stayed home to attend the University of Colorado's commuter campus in Colorado Springs. That year, I also started attending a booming megachurch called New Life Church, and boy did I ever start attending. When I wasn't in class, I was at church, listening to the sermons of Pastor Ted Haggard, New Life's founding pastor and rising star. When I wasn't at church, I was listening to his sermons on tape. I was reading the Bible in big, thirsty gulps. I was going to prayer groups with my new Christian friends.

After some years of teenage rebellion—drugs, booze, loads of lies to Mom and Dad—I'd done an about-face into religious zeal. I had, as I loved to say at the time, *rededicated my life to Christ.* I relished the sound of that phrase. I'd reoriented my entire sense of self, and I was happier than I'd ever been.

At twenty, for sophomore year, I transferred to Oral Roberts University (ORU) in Tulsa, Oklahoma. At ORU, classes opened in prayer, chapel was required twice a week, and every student spent a whole semester studying the Holy Spirit. I'd discovered the school through a pipeline between New Life Church and the university—Haggard was a graduate, as were other New Life pastors, and many of the people in the church's youth group went to ORU. I thought the school was a place where my raw, newfound faith would be rounded off.

Instead, it was lobbed off. It happened like the flip of a switch—one day while sitting in a chapel service, I felt my light of faith go dim. The mid-1990s were an era of experimental revivalism in North America, and ORU was a locus of it, complete with people laughing for hours on end and barking like dogs on the chapel floor—purported signs of the presence of the Holy Spirit. It was in such a service that I looked around at everyone acting out these godly extremes and, for a rare moment, trusted my gut: *Bullshit.* Some critical Christians are capable of leaving the baby in the bathwater, but for me, in the weeks and months that followed, faith dwindled down to a puddle. One question led to another. How had I not noticed how confusing the Bible could be? Why wouldn't preachers explain the most vexing verses? How could I trust that the invisible God I was reaching for was actually there? How could I be sure we weren't all making him up? I asked all my friends to pray for me. I read all the C. S. Lewis I could handle. But nothing would refill the tub again.

It took me years to connect my existential pendulum shifts to anything else in my story—to my father, for starters, and how unstable was the ground beneath my feet. It took me years to connect any of this to the lawn mower story or to having the alcoholic father veil pulled from my eyes at seventeen—how could I trust myself to know anything? It took me years to understand that spiritual doubt is a way of seeking, natural and necessary in any life of faith. At the time, all I knew was that I once was lost, then I was found, then I was lost again.

So, at twenty-one, I transferred schools again for my junior year, seeking secular shade at CSU. But I grieved my loss of faith. For much of that year, I was reeling, sick with uncertainty. I'd wake with swirlies in my stomach. I'd try to summon up enough belief to pray and, failing, angst my way through the day. An English major, I read my assigned texts with anxiety, worried that Virginia Woolf and Ernest Hemingway could do further damage to my soul. I'd try going back to the Bible, but now it was a question book more than an answer book. I struggled to eat, losing 12 or so pounds from my 6-foot, 150-pound frame. I should have seen a therapist, but such a notion would not occur to me, or be recommended to me, for many more years.

But I did have Mom. In this season of back-and-forth faith and doubt, she became my primary confidant and confessor. We talked multiple times a week, and I told her everything. I confessed my doubts, and I confessed my sins. I'd bump into old high school friends on campus, get invited to their parties, have an all-night trip down memory lane with their plentiful pot and Fat Tire, then call Mom the next day and tell her about my backslide. I'd tell her about making out with a random girl.

"Do you like her?" Mom would ask.

"Not really," I'd say.

"How do you think she feels about you?" she'd ask. I'd tell her that was a good question.

I'd talk about how I knew I was displeasing God but also ask, why should I feel that way? Are we sure God exists? How could we possibly know? If he is real, why does he insist on us finding him in this ancient book that no one understands? Have you read the end of the Book of Jonah, Mom? What the heck is going on there? What about the Gospel of Mark? Why is Jesus so cryptic and snippy?

We had a lot of phone calls like this. That's what we were doing on that Saturday morning in the winter of my junior year. Mom listened for a while, like always. Then she offered her suggestion: Find yourself a man.

"You have so many questions, son. You need someone to help you dig into them. And I know your dad has been . . . ," she trailed off. "You need another older, wiser man in your life. Don't you think that would be good?"

Mom reminded me of two men who had been in my life for a season during my teenage years—a Southern Baptist youth pastor named Rick and a boss at Chick-fil-A named John. She reminded me that I'd really looked up to them, learned a lot from them. Remember how helpful they were? She was right. I adored those guys, soaked up their every ounce of attention.

"You have so many questions," Mom said a second time. "I just think you would gain so much from an older man you could get close to. Maybe try a church? Or a Christian college group on campus. You have" (third time) "so many questions."

• • •

Mom had a nice way of making herself heard. I took her advice to heart. I began to think on the regular about how to solve the older man absence in my life. But I was not sure where to begin.

On two separate occasions—and I swear this is true—I tried finding a man in the halls of the CSU English Department. If I needed wisdom, what could be better than someone who had a PhD in literature? I went to the English Department expressly for that purpose, figuring that if I lingered in the hallway long enough, some kind professor would invite me into his office. He'd tell me about his favorite books, then we'd get into movies and music, and from there it'd be only natural to speak of his family and his upbringing and his core beliefs, all the things that made him *him*. Soon he'd ask me to coffee. Then dinner at the house, where he might have a wife and kids. Over dinner, we'd talk about Jane Austen, then maybe Woody Allen and the Coen Brothers. In time, he'd teach me to fly-fish, work on a budget, make a fire with sticks. He'd be my Papa Friend.

Apart from an awkward interaction with a British lit professor who seemed irritated that I hadn't yet read any Charles Dickens, I got zero nibbles in two tries at the English Department. A fool's errand, that, especially since what Mom really was imploring me to do was to find a man of God, and those are hard to come by in an English department. It's what I wanted, too, in spite of my rank skepticism. I missed having access to deep, all-day-everyday faith. I wanted it back.

For the next couple of months, I tried attending Christian groups on campus—Young Life, Campus Crusade for Christ (now called Cru), InterVarsity. I figured these groups would be a target-rich environment of older guys who wanted to mentor younger guys. And so they were. I met those guys, but I was all angst, and they were all earnest. I wore my spiritual questions like heavy robes, and every praise song and Bible study session was like water falling on those robes. I sagged under the weight. Everyone at those groups seemed to have some basic feeling for God that I somehow could no longer attain. Being there made me feel more confused and alone.

CSU's Christian scene wasn't for me, but perhaps actual churches would be? Maybe I could find a New Life Church comp in Fort Collins? For several weeks straight that semester, I rode my bike to a different church each week: nondenominational, Baptist, Lutheran, Methodist, Vineyard, Catholic. Each week, I rode away more perplexed than before. Were these churches even the same religion? Was it worth trying to get used to them in order to start a relationship where shared faith would be the price of entry?

Every now and then, I'd go home to Colorado Springs for a weekend visit. My church there remained the one place where God really made sense. Whenever I went home, I'd go to a New Life service or two and, at the very least, experience some semblance of faith.

Pastor Ted Haggard sometimes brought in preachers from around the country. He had set a high bar for his pulpit, and if he brought in a guest speaker, you knew he (almost always a he) was someone Haggard knew could clear that bar. One Sunday night, the bar-clearing preacher was a missionary from Mexico named David Hogan. I'd heard of Hogan many times—he was something of a legend in those parts, but I'd never had a chance to listen to him speak.

That night, I found out that David Hogan couldn't just clear the bar; he could put it in his hands, cock it like a baseball bat, and swing it right into my teeth.

Hogan had a bushy head of hair and a thick beard. He wore cowboy boots, Wrangler jeans, and a button-down shirt with pearl snaps, like he'd ridden to the service on horseback. For decades, Hogan told us, he'd lived in remote parts of Mexico, traipsing through the hills preaching the gospel of Jesus Christ and performing the signs and wonders that he said followed any genuine presentation of the gospel. He'd seen people healed from all manner of diseases. He said he'd even seen a boy raised from the dead through the power of prayer.

I did not know if any of that was true, but it sure *sounded* true. It *felt* true, when Hogan said it. As he talked, I began to imagine how being with him might change my life. If I followed this man to Mexico, I would no longer have to doubt. I could see the miraculous work of God firsthand. I would no longer have to look for a father figure, because Hogan was the manliest man I'd ever seen. He exuded confidence and strength but spoke of compassion and mercy. He was the full package. I began to fantasize about what it would be like to actually know him and for him to know me.

Later, I heard Hogan was coming back to Colorado Springs to preach again, and I made sure to be there. He preached for an hour that night, then prayed over people in the service for another hour. Everyone he prayed for trembled and wept; some of them crumpled to the ground. I stood in line for him to lay his hands on me, and when he did, I tried hard to feel something. I stuck around as the hour got late and waited for Hogan to finish praying for everyone else. Then I walked up to him and shot my shot.

"I want to come to Mexico," I said. "I want to join the work you're doing there."

"I don't do missionary trips," he said. "I do missionary life."

"That's what I want," I said.

He stared at me for a serious moment, sizing me up.

"I'm rough and tumble," he said. "We fast all the time. We get around on horseback and foot. It's a hard life."

"I'm ready for all of that," I said.

He stared at me again, hard and long, so long that I can still feel him staring today. Finally, he spoke again.

"Pray about it for six months. If you still want to come, write me a letter."

I waited six months and then wrote a letter to the address he'd given me, a PO box located at the Texas border. I dreamed of living the rest of my life under his wing. I let my questions rage, trusting that they'd all be answered by David Hogan someday.

For months on end, I kept checking my mailbox for hand-scribbled envelopes from Mexico.

In the interim, some salves appeared in my life that throttled my father-figure-seeking. While shooting hoops one day, I befriended a slightly older guy named Peder who seemed to have his act together—he had a job, owned a house, checked in on his parents regularly, talked about balancing his checkbook and making something called "investments." He was a full-grown adult person. He was also a Christian with loads of questions about Christianity, but he seemed to wear them easily, like a thrifted T-shirt.

Then, one of my roommates, Amy, invited me to a new church she was attending, and there I met a pastor named Kyle Parker, who was also just a few years older than I was and who had been tasked with starting a new college group. Like Peder, he wasn't father-figure material yet, but he cut a father-like figure—broad and tall like a house, with a deep, booming voice that made him seem even larger. He'd recently gotten married, which made him seem even older. Kyle told me his entire job was to help college students navigate college life.

A few days later, Kyle and I were sitting across from each other in a coffee shop on the CSU campus. He was the best listener I'd encountered in a long time—he didn't simplify questions, and he wasn't threatened by them. After I talked about all my doubts for a while, he responded by asking if I wanted to join the leadership team of his new campus ministry.

"Did you hear any of what I just said?" I asked him. "I don't even know what I believe. I can't read three Bible verses without curling into a ball of doubt."

"I like your questions," he said. "I think you're going to sort them out over time. I want someone like you on my team."

I joined his team. I learned to do things like plan retreats, organize group hikes, make chili for large groups of people.

Kyle kept making lots of room for my doubt. Sometimes I would even catch a new wave of faith, and whenever it came, I'd try to ride that wave as long as I could. When it crashed, Kyle would gently bring me to shore. He put real effort into getting to know me, which should have been a clue about what I really needed in a father figure.

Through Kyle, I met another slightly older guy, Joshua, and we became fast friends. Joshua talked about his dad a lot. He did it naturally, the way you'd talk about a friend who said funny and insightful things all the time. I marked it, marveled at it. He told stories of the cabin he had helped his dad build. Through his stories, I felt like I was getting some fathering by osmosis. Through his friendship, I found comfort and safety, which should also have been a clue about what I needed in a father figure.

Another year passed, with no response from Hogan. During this period, Mom's health insurance plan at her job got upgraded to full dental coverage. She called me to say that she could finally afford to put me in the braces that we could never afford when I was little (thanks to years of inveterate thumb-sucking up until I was seven or eight, my teeth were crooked on top and crowded below). We went through a couple of rounds of prep with an orthodontist, and I learned about the years it would take to fix my mouth. When it came time to schedule the appointment to get the braces on, I backed out. What if David Hogan wrote back? What if he invited me into his ministry? I didn't want American braces to be the reason I couldn't go live in rural Mexico with a man of God.

Another year passed. I fell in love with a fellow English major named Michaela. I was scheduled to graduate in the fall of 1997, but I unenrolled in a class or two so that I could stay in college an extra semester to be with Michaela. I did not mention to her that I might be a missionary in Mexico someday. I did not mention it to anyone.

Finally, in the spring of 1998, a few weeks before my college graduation, I came home one day to find a letter from David Hogan. He said I was welcome to come to Mexico. He gave me instructions for setting up a visit. I stood in my kitchen holding the letter, touching base with the version of myself that had been ready to give my life to this man a couple of years before.

I still believed I needed a man like Hogan. But there had to be another way. I was in love with the woman I wanted to marry. I had big-brotherly friends. I read the letter again, then slipped it into the trash.

My teeth are still crooked.

8

The Pastor

IF YOU'VE BEEN following American religion and politics news over the last couple of decades, you may have raised your eyebrows at a certain name in the last chapter: Ted Haggard, the founding pastor of the church I began attending as a teenager in Colorado Springs. From the 1990s through the mid-aughts, Pastor Ted, as he was known, was a lot of people's idea of a model evangelical leader. President George W. Bush's White House included Pastor Ted in its list of West Wing advisors. In 2003, he was asked to lead the National Association of Evangelicals and represent its millions of members. In 2005, *Time* magazine featured him in a cover story entitled "The 25 Most Influential Evangelicals in America." Pastor Ted was considered a breath of fresh evangelical air—against same-sex marriage, yes, but also pro–civil unions, pro-environment, pro-economic development on behalf of the poor. In a time of ideological hardening, Pastor Ted had a knack for relative nuance. He was a big evangelical deal who seemed poised to become much bigger.

But his prominence peaked in scandal. In 2006, a masseur in Denver claimed to have sold Pastor Ted methamphetamine and engaged with him in sexual activity. The pastor lost his church and his leadership positions, and he began to recede from public view. Today, unless you're a religion and politics nerd, you've likely never heard of him.

That is to the good—for the ministries that he founded and, I imagine, for him and his family. The limelight is a vexing place to be.

Scandals like Pastor Ted's come and go, but the limelight is not long in wanting the next one—a popular pastor rises, a popular pastor falls. In the handful of weeks I've been drafting this chapter, two high-profile Christian leaders have been outed for various sexual and financial abuses. When such fresh news breaks, my mind always goes to the many sincere followers these men (almost always men) leave in the wake of their scandal. The people who found their teaching helpful, life-shaping, even salvific. The people whose trust and admiration the pastors worked hard to earn. The people who saw them as father figures. Read the comment threads on these stories and you'll see such people scoffed at, called "sheep." Which, yes, that's exactly what they are, because it's what they're aiming to be—sheep following a shepherd, as the Bible tells them so.

A good shepherd is hard to find. It's also hard to become. As job complexity goes, pastoring is underrated. The position requires a daunting mix of hard and soft skills. You gotta be able to understand the Bible (no small feat) and make it interesting to a cross section of humans. You gotta be able to relate to rich and poor, sick and healthy, old and young. You gotta have organizational chops, overseeing human resources, accounting, strategic planning, event planning, crowd control, building maintenance. Pastoring is hard as hell.

Ted Haggard grew a church of over ten thousand people because he had pastoring skills in spades. In his heyday, Pastor Ted was a ringer. People who arrived at New Life Church were captivated by a charming, intelligent man who talked plain sense about God. Is your Bible boring and impenetrable? In Pastor Ted's hands, it became fascinating and approachable. Is your God distant and judgy? In Pastor Ted's telling, God was folksy, friendly, and eager to save you.

Pastor Ted's core Scripture was perhaps Genesis 3, the story of the garden of Eden. God creates the first human couple and places them in a garden with two fruit trees. One is the tree of life, and its fruits will provide harmony, joy, an easy-going way. The other is the tree of the knowledge of good and evil, and its fruits lead to self-absorption, confusion, and conflict. Pastor Ted taught that each of us faces a two-tree binary every day. We can choose to be "life-giving"—his favorite term—to ourselves and everyone around us. Or we can try to nourish ourselves with short-term, self-focused pleasures. Pastor Ted presented Christianity as a life-giving way of life.

But the gospel he preached was not just about you. New Life Church was a kind of newsroom—week in and week out, you'd hear about events all over the world, from Washington, DC to Kiev, Ukraine, to Baku, Azerbaijan. Flags of the world's nations hung from the sanctuary ceiling—reminders that there were people out there going through all sorts of things and that those people needed God. In the main, nothing coming from the pulpit seemed too political or partisan—it was just engaged, informed. Pastor Ted would tell you to read two things every morning: the Bible and the morning paper. Then, you were to take the morning paper and wrap it around your Bible like a gift. And the Bible *was* a gift—its wisdom and power could intervene in all those news reports of conflict and suffering. To hear Pastor Ted tell it, God's spirit was constantly roaming the earth and seeking ways to lead people to life, to prevent darkness from spreading. When Christians prayed for the world, they were participating in the roaming, life-giving work of God.

When I heard this message in the mid-1990s as a teenager at New Life Church, it was the stuff of revelation. Pastor Ted made Christianity seem like a well-made frame inside of which everything fit. His teaching reset my entire life, my entire understanding of what life is. It helped me look beyond myself and sense a call to service. For a young man of eighteen and nineteen desperate to make sense of the world, Pastor Ted was, well, a godsend.

Then, for a confused young man of twenty-one, twenty-two, twenty-three in search of a father figure, Pastor Ted became something like a Papa Friend. He was in my head a lot in those days—an ideal, an image of a life well lived. I listened to his sermons on tape over and over, even (perhaps especially) when I wasn't sure if I still believed. I thought of what it'd be like to know him and be known by him. I'd talked to him a handful of times over the years—even with a church of thousands, he was pretty approachable. But he also existed in the stratosphere. He was a model of the kind of man I wanted in my life, not an actual option. Anyway, I no longer lived in Colorado Springs and didn't have any desire to. (That's where Dad lived, after all.)

Which is why it felt like something of a miracle—an intervention of God—when out of the blue, a couple of months after college graduation, I learned that Pastor Ted was in need of a writer. It's why I leapt at the chance to become that writer. It's why I did my best to convince Pastor Ted that I was ready, that I could commit to the job fully, that it didn't matter what he paid me or even what the work exactly entailed. I was all-in. It's why I decided to take the job and move back to Colorado Springs without consulting a single person about the decision—including the woman I was about to marry.

• • •

Michaela and I fell in love over the course of my last year at CSU. Me first—I'd had a crush on her for months, while she didn't know me from Adam. I set about trying to change that by figuring out where she'd be on campus at any given time of day. ("I'm seeing you everywhere this semester," she said at one point. "I know! So weird!" I replied.) I finally worked up the courage to ask her out, and she said yes to a Saturday morning hike, thinking that I was inviting her to a group hike, not a date hike. (I may have been deliberately vague.) I heard about her mistake through a roommate who knew one of Michaela's roommates, and every time my house phone rang that week, I worried it was Michaela calling to cancel. She did not, and so on that Saturday morning I picked her up in my freshly scrubbed 1985 Jeep Wagoneer and took her to a favorite trail.

Within the first two miles of that first hike, I was convinced I wanted to be in Michaela's company for as long as she would have me. I still feel that way this morning, even as she sleeps in our bedroom upstairs.

Eight months after that hike, in May 1998, we were engaged. I would graduate a week later, but Michaela still had one semester of school to finish. We didn't have much of a plan for what we'd do when she graduated—master's degrees for both of us at some point, probably at CSU. Mostly we just wanted to stay put and start building our lives. We loved Fort Collins and could not imagine leaving anytime soon. That summer, she had a line on a summer job in Colorado Springs, but I convinced her to stay in Fort Collins with me so we could go ahead and begin building the life we'd be living together after we were married.

I was working as a nurse aid for Medicare, as I'd done throughout college, but I desperately wanted to work with words. I began to apply for every writing-related job I could find in the area. I got no traction from the local newspaper, a radio station, or a puny publisher. After a few weeks of swings and misses, I went home to Colorado Springs for a quick visit with my mom and (okay, fine) dad. While there, I had coffee with a friend, John Bolin, who was the youth pastor at New Life Church. I shared my woes. I told him I had a fiancé who had one semester of college left. I had a father-in-law-to-be who was asking good but terrifying questions about what I planned to do for a living. I had no prospects and, I was beginning to fear, no employable skills.

John was a problem-solving pastor. Tell him your challenges, and he'll start brainstorming solutions on the spot. I knew he'd have a thought or two. John also had a side hustle, probably five side hustles—he was an innate entrepreneur, and I figured he'd help me think outside the box about ways to make money in Fort Collins.

But John had a different idea.

"You can write, right?"

"I guess so," I said.

"I know so," he said. "You know who needs a writer?"

"Who?"

"Pastor Ted. His star is on the rise. He's got more writing opportunities than he can handle." John said the church was on its way to ten thousand members. Pastor Ted would be among the next big evangelical leaders, not just in Colorado but in the nation. Maybe the world. He'd be someone magazines profiled, TV shows called for sit-downs. He'd be invited to speak all over the planet. He would go, go, go, go, go.

He was becoming, John said, someone many publishers wanted to publish. Pastor Ted had just written his first book, and sales were brisk. He would need a full-time writer. He needed one even now.

My head was spinning. John knew he was sharing good news, but he had no idea all the news I was hearing. Pastor Ted was not just an answer to prayers for a job. He could be the answer to my mom's prayers for me. Hell, to *my* prayers for me. He could be the father figure to end all father figures. I hardly knew how to handle all the good news coming out of John's mouth.

From that coffee with John, things happened fast.

Pastor Ted called the next morning.

"Patton! I hear you're in town and that you're a writer."

"Yes! Well, that's what I want to be."

"Me too!" he said and laughed. He said he'd been working on a magazine article and wasn't happy with it. "Do you want to take a look and see if you can fix it?"

"Of course," I said. "When?"

"How about now?"

I drove to the church straightaway and found my way to Pastor Ted's office. He handed me his laptop and pointed me to a space where I could work for a quiet hour. He left while I edited the article into shape, then came by and read it in front of me. He said it was good work. Was I interested in doing this full-time? Yes and please and thank you. How much money would I need? I said I had no idea. He said to sit down with my fiancé, figure out what it would take to cover our monthly bills, and let him know.

My fiancé! Right! I had one of those.

I had yet to mention any of this to Michaela. *Any of this*—including New Life Church and Ted Haggard. I mean, she knew a bit about my religious history. She knew I'd *rededicated my life to Christ* at a big church in Colorado Springs after high school. But it's not like we talked about it all that much. It's not like I'd played her my Pastor Ted sermon tapes. It's certainly not like I'd told her I'd been on a years-long search for a Papa Friend. I kept that stuff to myself.

But wow . . . she was going to be so excited for me. *So excited.* For sure. No doubt. She'd love this idea. *Love it.*

I drove the two hours back to Fort Collins. Michaela was still at work, so I figured I might as well use the time to pack. I went home and started gathering all my earthly possessions—one chair, one lamp, some clothes, a Broncos blanket, a snowboard, many books. I piled everything into the back of my Wagoneer, then headed to Michaela's house. She was going to be so surprised! So happy for me! I had a writing job! And it started right away! In beautiful Colorado Springs! What an exciting turn of events for us!

Michaela's response did not quite match my expectations.

She had many questions, beginning with, Who is Ted Haggard? And what is a megachurch? What is a ghostwriter? What would you write about? Are you supposed to write sermons? Tell me again, what is a megachurch? Do they have to call it that? Would we have to go to church there every Sunday? What do they teach? Is it anything like any other church she'd ever gone to? Did I really think she'd like it, or did I just want to convince her to like it?

Also, was I moving *now*? How could I possibly do that without talking to her? After convincing her to spend the summer in Fort Collins? How could I have already packed my car?

I did not yet know some things that are obvious to me now. Like: life-changing decisions are not good surprises. And: people in a relationship should not make decisions that involve (1) place, (2) money, and (3) religion without consulting each other. That was about as obvious to me as where to put oil in a lawn mower.

In my mind, the deed was done, and I could not imagine undoing it. I persuaded Michaela to come down to Colorado Springs for a visit. Go to church with me. Meet Pastor Ted in person. She'd see that he was pretty great. She'd see that this job was an open door I'd be crazy not to walk through. She'd see that with Pastor Ted, I'd be getting far more than a boss. I'd be getting a man who would settle my questions, guide my wandering heart, and show me how to live.

Didn't she want to be married to someone who knew how to live?

The next weekend, Michaela drove down to Colorado Springs and we visited New Life Church for the Sunday morning service. We sat in the middle row of a packed section near the megachurch stage, praise and worship music booming, people raising hands to God and jump-dancing in the aisles.

I could tell that Michaela was eyeing the exits. She'd never experienced a worship service quite like this—loud, dancy—and it was overwhelming for her. I told myself to be patient. Once she had a chance to talk to Pastor Ted, he'd put her at ease. It would all be okay.

After the service, we waited around near the megachurch stage while Pastor Ted prayed for all the people who wanted prayer and chatted with all the people who wanted chatting. Finally, he turned to us and greeted Michaela with his big, warm smile.

"So what do you think?" he said to her. "Is God calling Patton to come write for me?"

"Oh, I'm not sure," she admitted.

"Well, we think he is," he assured her. "We're excited to see what God is going to do."

This is all going so well! I thought.

We chatted for a few moments more, then said goodbye. Pastor Ted said he'd be in touch with final details of salary and start date.

As we walked out of the sanctuary, I could hardly wait for Michaela's response. Okay, so maybe the church's worship service style wasn't her favorite. But Ted's charisma was infectious. He was kind and generous. His confidence in me was palpable. He'd not used the *God calling Patton* phrase with me before, but I felt those words underscored the moment, the opportunity, and yes, the calling. That's what this was—not just a job offer but a God offer.

We walked in silence to the car. We got inside, me in the driver's seat and her in shotgun. I turned to Michaela.

"So, what do you think? He's pretty great, right?"

Michaela looked out her window for a long moment, then back at me.

"I think there's something off about him," she said.

• • •

We talked about it for hours. We talked about it for days, weeks, years. We don't talk about it anymore, because so much life has accumulated on top of that decision. So much change for both of us. It's astonishing to consider who you were at twenty-three, to revisit the crossroads of your life and recall which way you thought was right and which way you thought was wrong. Whom you trusted. Who you thought needed persuading. What you asked—or insisted—of the people who loved you most.

Michaela is an incisive person, observant and sharp. I've learned over the years that when we disagree, I best pay close attention to what she's saying. I've learned to strain to listen to her signal piercing my noise. She's not always right, as none of us are. But when Michaela and I are in conflict, and especially when we're at crossroad moments, I am well advised to consider the way she wants to lead. Her instincts are trustworthy.

I did not know that about her in 1998. For all my insecurity, I did not know how to check myself, to let someone shine a light down alternative paths. So I walked the only path I could see: I took the job and waited for Michaela to come around. I believed—though I did not say it—that men should make these decisions. The decision about where I'd work and where we'd live was finally mine to make, because I was a man. I would be a provider. I would be the spiritual leader in my home. My father had not been either of those things, but I would be those things. The Lord—especially now, with Pastor Ted as my guide—would make me a man.

I moved back into my parents' house and started my new job. Michaela stayed behind in Fort Collins to wait for her final semester of school to begin. Throughout the remaining months of our engagement, we wrestled with what I had done and what it would mean for our lives. She came to New Life some weekends and started trying to get used to it, but the church was a far cry from anywhere she wanted to be. I was determined to make it our home. One night, we drove around talking for hours, then parked at an overlook and sat up until nearly dawn, exploring the chasm between our perspectives. Could we bridge it? Did it still make sense for us to get married? It was one of the hardest, scariest conversations of my life.

Michaela joined me in Colorado Springs five months after I started working for Pastor Ted—two weeks after she graduated from college, one week after we were married.

I had it all: a full-time writing job, a wife I adored, and a boss who was also my pastor and who would also be the father figure I'd been seeking all along.

9

Figure Out

EIGHT YEARS LATER, early in the fall of 2006, I sat in my living room and typed out a letter to Pastor Ted. I'd resigned from New Life a few months before. He had offered me a generous exit ramp of continued salary while we wrapped up a few projects. Before we reached the end of that ramp, I wanted to set the record of our relationship straight.

I cannot find a copy of that emailed letter today, and I will not attempt a reproduction. But I believe I remember the spirit of it. I was grateful for the education in professional writing that the job had provided—we'd completed six books together, written op-eds, composed letters, workshopped conference presentations. The job had also provided considerable flexibility. In 2001, two years into my New Life tenure, Michaela and I moved across the country so I could start a PhD program at Boston University (BU). We moved back four years later, after our first child was born. Pastor Ted had kept me gainfully employed all along. And I loved the church staff, counting several people there among my dearest friends.

But New Life was never the homecoming I'd hoped it would be. It took some years to admit—mostly to myself—that Michaela had been right, even though it became clear almost immediately. I struggled to find my place at the church even as I ghostwrote for the senior pastor. Some of the young men on staff managed to get a lot of time with him, but I never could quite figure out how to be in that inner circle. And deep down, I knew I didn't belong and never would. I was yet a long time in coming to terms with that unbelonging.

My crisis of faith wasn't helped by working for a church. If anything, the job sharpened the pangs of doubt. Belief was a job requirement, and I learned to live with cognitive dissonance. When working on Pastor Ted's books, I adopted his perspective as best I could. I listened to his sermon tapes over and over. I read the Bible with his eyes, pushing my questions aside. In my second year on the job, I developed a wicked case of insomnia, sometimes going three or four nights at a time with virtually no sleep. I'd sit up all night, staring into the middle distance. I'd drop to my knees and ask God to help, please help, please just please give me my simple faith back, make everything click in. I decided to read the Bible from cover to cover and write down every question that occurred to me, thinking if I could order my doubts, I could address them, one by one. I hoped I would come around.

I began to explore other Christianities, catching a scent of other ways to think about God and Jesus and the Bible. I read Flannery O'Connor, Martin Luther King Jr., Walker

Percy, Annie Dillard, Frederick Buechner. Their understandings of the faith felt like a whole other religion, one that was pained and complex but inviting and whole. Michaela and I began to go to two services on Sunday—first an Episcopalian Eucharist, then New Life's charismatic worship. In my third year on staff, I moved all the way to Boston to study religion. I crammed my head with voices and perspectives across the ages. Even so, every time Pastor Ted would call to discuss a writing project, I would immediately flip back to his point of view. It didn't even feel hard to make that leap of faith whenever we talked—I still wanted to be in his world or at least in his favor. I wrote things I did not believe, not for a paycheck but for continued connection to Pastor Ted.

I also wrote for myself. I quietly published articles—in small magazines well outside New Life's purview—that critiqued evangelical culture. Later, in my second year at BU, I wrote a memoir about my conversion experience at New Life and year at ORU, published in 2004 as *My Faith So Far: A Story of Conversion and Confusion*. I tried to thread the needle of the risk I was taking by including Ted on the dedication page, but I heard through the grapevine that Ted was hurt by what I'd written. I heard he was ready to let me go. I called him and persuaded him that he didn't need to do that—I was still on board with him and his ministry. I persuaded myself it was true.

For eight years, I wasn't ready to be let go. By the end, I was thirty-two years old, raising a family of my own, wrapping up a doctorate, side-hustling as a journalist, yet still I felt that I would only ever find myself in Ted's shadow. Maybe we could eventually talk to each other. Maybe he'd really want to get to know me. Maybe he'd see that, yes, I thought about things in a different way, but he'd be charmed by that difference. Maybe we'd come to an understanding, a mutual acceptance. Maybe I'd write for him for the rest of my life.

Even as I was finally moving on, in my letter in the fall of 2006 I assured Pastor Ted that whatever doubts I had were minor in comparison to one major fact I knew for certain: He remained for me an image of the father I'd never had.

When I first came to New Life Church as a high school senior, I wrote, *I was made in my father's image. Drinking and drugging, just like him. Insecure and mean-spirited. I did not know how to be life-giving. You and your ministry changed all that.*

You are the one who modeled for me what it means to be a man, I wrote. *You gave me my first vision of a life of faith and love.*

I love you as I would love a good father, I wrote, *because that is what you have been to me.*

• • •

Pastor Ted never responded. Which was surprising and odd—in spite of our tensions, he never ignored me. I figured I'd hear from him in hours, days at most. For weeks, Ted's silence worried me.

Then, one morning a month or so after I sent the letter, I woke up, made some coffee, and opened my laptop to read the morning news. When I saw the headline at the top of the local paper's website, I nearly dropped my mug into my lap: "New Life's Haggard Accused of Sex and Drugs Relationship."

A masseur in Denver was claiming that he'd sold Pastor Ted drugs. He said they'd had sexual encounters. Pastor Ted was quoted as denying everything. But within hours of the story breaking, some of us who were close to Pastor Ted began to get word that at least some of the accusations were true.

Strange numbers began to ring my phone. Serious voices left serious voicemails asking me to return their calls. It was the *New York Times*. It was *Good Morning America*. I was reeling, along with everyone else who knew Pastor Ted. I had no idea how to respond to these inquiries.

At some point that day, a journalist pal of mine called and encouraged me to speak with the *New York Times*' longtime religion reporter, Laurie Goodstein. I agreed to do it. She was a reporter I'd always respected, and I knew she'd take care with the story. I sat on my couch, head in hands, as Laurie asked the questions she needed to ask. Did we see this coming? No. Was this a secret anyone else knew about? I don't think so. Did I think Pastor Ted was a closeted gay man? I doubted it was that simple.

As we wrapped up, Laurie had a suggestion. "If you don't want to talk about this story, you should probably turn off your phone. It's about to get crazy."

No sooner had I hung up the phone than *Good Morning America* called again. A producer told me they wanted to come to my house later that day and shoot a segment. Was I willing to do that?

I paused. I muffled a sob. "I really don't think so," I said. "I am nowhere close to being able to talk about this on camera."

The woman was quiet for a moment. Then she started speaking in a near whisper. "Listen," she said. "People like me are all over this story. We're ringing your phone now, but soon we are going to be knocking on your front door. If you really don't want to talk about it, you need to gather your family and go to a hotel for a few days."

Instead, I called my editor at Beliefnet, the religion journalism outlet based in New York City, where I'd recently taken an editorial position. The company's PR firm came to the rescue, creating a firewall for interview requests, a kindness I'll never forget.

A few hours later, my phone rang with a number I recognized. Ted Haggard was calling.

"Patton, I'm so sorry," he sobbed. He said that he had been running so hard for so long, traveling all over the world nonstop, and that he had just collapsed. He had self-destructed for a little while, eaten from the tree of the knowledge of good and evil. He told me he never meant to hurt anyone. He said he was getting the help he needed. He would be better soon.

We cried together for a few moments, exchanging words of concern.

"I'm sorry I never responded to your letter," he said. "It broke my heart to read it. I knew this storm was coming. I knew you were about to be disappointed by another father figure."

• • •

The Pastor Ted story had legs. Much of the immediate media interest was focused on his sexuality—whether he was gay, straight, or somewhere in between. How he was a "biblical marriage" hypocrite. Pastor Ted handled the issue variously over time, saying he was at neither end of the Kinsey scale, that he was "heterosexual but with issues," then "completely heterosexual." For a few years, every new utterance from him on the matter brought a fresh round of coverage.

Other angles proliferated—the pitfalls of megachurch Christianity, patriarchal religious leadership, evangelicals and power. What happens to a church when its pastor becomes a national and international figure? What happens when evangelical faith is leveraged for political gain? Many pieces of Pastor Ted–focused media were made in the years that followed the scandal—TV broadcasts, an HBO documentary, YouTube assessments, a *GQ* profile, NPR programs, podcasts, op-eds, academic studies. I wrote a handful of pieces myself.

But I also declined more significant chances to weigh in. In that first hot year after the scandal, I was offered life-changing money and platforms for a deeper exposé on Pastor Ted. I turned them down, and it wasn't hard. Pastor Ted had become human to me long before the scandal, and I knew he was more complicated than his scandal suggested. I could sooner imagine writing a nonfiction novel than I could an exposé.

I thought a lot about the light that made the shadow side possible. Pastor Ted was not just a pastor who had a fall from grace. He was a man who spent years—and no doubt still is, in whatever ways he can find—responding to what he believed was the call of God on his life. He planted a church that, whatever else it was, became an institution that altered the life course of many people, including yours truly. That, too, is part of his legacy. All those things I said to Pastor Ted about him being the one who first showed me how to be life-giving? Still true.

Yet a scandal is a kind of *apocalypse*, not in the sense of a world-ending event but in the term's original sense, which is *revelation*. I'm speaking not of what hits the news but of the private unveiling, the big rethinking that happens in living rooms and at dinner tables among those who are close to a charismatic and complicated public figure. In the months and years following November 2006, I had more honest conversations with people around New Life Church than I'd ever had. I learned that I was not the only one who had been father-figuring Pastor Ted, far from it. I was also not the only one who had felt plagued by questions, yet too insecure to really ask them. I was not the only one who had remained in the mix despite my changing theological and political convictions. I was in better company than I knew.

A scandal is a piercing, a breaking of a spell. I'd been under one for most of a decade, and I'd been my own wizard—my own heart and mind had been casting it on me. I knew within my first year at New Life Church that I was a bad fit. I knew I wasn't aligned enough, that I was hungry—desperate, even—for a different expression of religion, if I still wanted any religion at all. But I could never trust my own instincts. My insecurity was a winch that kept pulling me back in.

In time, through the guidance of friends and therapists and spiritual directors, I realized there could have been another version of my story. Several options occurred to me that I'd never thought of before. I could have offered to write for Pastor Ted while building the life Michaela and I wanted in Fort Collins. I could have proposed a trial period—that we try writing a first book together, see how it goes. I could have, at some point over those last eight years, been honest with Pastor Ted about my questions and my critique. I could have dared intellectual integrity. But I never approached him directly about any of it. I was too insecure. I labored for years under the illusion that without a connection to Pastor Ted, I had little hope of becoming who I needed to be.

The scandal set me free of all that. It broke the spell. I began to believe a new story about who I am.

I also began to believe a new story about who I needed in my life. I still needed guides and, yes, father figures. But my relationship with Pastor Ted had been a figment of my imagination. He was a Papa Friend. I never once had dinner at his home. I barely knew his wife and children, and he never knew mine. I was his employee, not his son or even his mentee.

This is no complaint. The expectations I had for our relationship were mine alone. Most bosses don't build complex emotional bonds with their employees, and well they shouldn't. Pastor Ted had a big organization to run, thousands of people who wanted his attention, speaking engagements far and wide. Still, it is simply and unavoidably confusing to have a boss who is also your pastor who is also the person whose teaching changed your life and the person you most want to be your father figure—the person who will not only teach you but also know you. Join you along your way. The relationship is overloaded—spiritually, emotionally, professionally—and it's almost impossible for it not to sink.

For all their *Good to Great* striving, modern churches are not just professional nonprofit organizations; they are also family systems whose aura of leadership is parental in nature. As an employee, you find value not just in your job function but in how you're seen and treated by the pastor. You might feel like a favored son or daughter, or you might feel like a black sheep. These dynamics make the employer-employee, pastor-parishioner relationship pretty damn confusing.

There are saving graces, though. Despite my—and our entire community's—preoccupation with Pastor Ted, the reality is that I was living in a world of people who were down for some father-figuring. Megachurches are lousy with them, as well as sisters and brothers and fellow travelers of all kinds. Even in my earliest, angstiest days at New Life, when I couldn't get the access to Pastor Ted I wanted, I found other guides. There were other people who would take me under their wings or at least take me out to lunch and listen to my many questions. Entire hallways were full of people—pastors, peers, secretaries, interns—who were eager to get personal, to talk about anything and everything.

I also broadened my network over time. I found a priest named Father Michael, who helped me reimagine who and what God is. A local journalist named Steve had me over to his house all the time for wandering conversations and good counsel. My wife's boss, Glenn, was a quiet powerhouse philosopher who taught both Michaela and me to ask better and more fruitful questions. One of the New Life pastors, Joseph, got me involved with a national community of Christian intellectuals who broadened my horizons.

I'd created, or been given, Papa Friend in the aggregate.

But I couldn't see all this until the spell was broken.

Every now and then, I'll meet someone who is in thrall to an older man or woman. I can tell they've been doing some father-figuring or mother-figuring—they've put themselves in someone's shadow. If I have an opening, I'll tell them to take a chance on stepping outside the shadow. Get to know their own mind. Realize that however charismatic and wise that person is, however helpful they've been, they're almost certainly holding them in too high regard. Bring them down to size. Break the spell.

That's easier said than done. Father figures, like the fathers who come before them, will have a hold on you. When you make yourself someone's child, part of you hopes they'll see you that way, care for you that way, no matter how unreasonable or hopeless your expectation. But there is always a move to make: You can find more father figures. Put the person in a medley. Find more voices to listen to.

Mom had wanted me to find someone who could help me answer my many questions. I ended up finding many people, not to answer the questions, necessarily, but at least to join me in asking them. In the abundance of counselors, says the proverb, there is safety. *Abundance* is the operative word.

• • •

You might think that, approaching fifty, I'd have long since abandoned the search for father figures. It's true that I don't need a Papa Friend anymore. The ramshackle barns I pass now are just ramshackle barns. But I still take all the guidance I can get. I find it in all sorts of sources. I've got Michaela. I've got Kaysie. I've got a wise boss and brilliant colleagues. I've gone to therapy, and I will do so again. I've been seeing the same spiritual director for over a decade, and she has become a dear friend who is also a pastor and like a sister. I've got a deep and abiding community of friends. I have all the companions I need.

I've also come to terms with my own tendencies. I've accepted my father-figuring as a way of being. I used to think my aching need for guidance was a weakness, but now I regard it as a strength—I am a sponge of input. Every now and then, an older person says something wise to me, and I write it down. I note how some father or mother is treating their kids in a life station just up ahead of mine. If it seems healthy and wise, I mark it.

Mom prayed that I would find a man. But the answer to her prayer came in the form of many people.

Perhaps most of all, it came in the form of her.

Part 3

THE ONE YOU BELIEVE IN

In his ineffable essence he is father; in his compassion to us he became mother. The father by loving becomes feminine.

—St. Clement of Alexandria

God cannot be very far from someone honestly confronting his own experience.

—Howard E. Butt Jr.

10

Father God, Giver of Bikes

MY MOM LOVED to tell a story about the way I talked to God.

I was six or seven years old, and I wanted a bicycle. My big sister, Kaysie, who was eleven or twelve, had taught me to ride a bike, but we had only one Big Kid Bike between us. The world just outside our Tennessee home opened into wide streets, and Kaysie and the other neighborhood big kids were full-time riders of those streets, racing and wheelieing and leaping from plywood ramps. They invited me into their play sometimes, but I had a job to do—I'd lie down at the lip of those ramps, the last in a row of kids, as they'd gather enough speed and height and distance to try to sail over us.

Fine, happy to play along, but I wanted to be one of the kids gathering speed and height and trying to sail. Mom said I wanted a bike the way people want food and water. Dad was always out making money but bringing none back in, and I dared not bug him about my bikelessness. But to Mom I would speak on the regular of the bike-shaped hole in my life.

"Patton, I'd love for you to have a bike," she would respond. "That's just not something we can do right now."

Then—and this was Mom's favorite part of the story—I would look up at her and say, "That's okay, Mom. If it is God's will, he will give me one." At night when she tucked me in and we said our prayers, I would remind God how things worked between us: "Father God, I really want a bike. I know we can't get me one, but I also know that you *can* get me one, if it is your will."

Mom loved my *not my will, but yours be done* take on bike prayers. My faith was so simple and pure that it encouraged her own faith, she said. But she also worried that my trust in God was going to lead to disappointment, because she could not see how a bike would be coming my way anytime soon. She worried that I'd start asking questions. Why would a good God not want a kid to have a bike?

One random day, there was a knock at our front door. Mom opened it to a strange man standing outside.

"Is this the Dodd residence?" he asked.

"Yes, it is," she said.

"I came by to give you this." He handed her a little yellow envelope. "I know there is a little boy here who is praying for a bicycle. Take this money. Let him go pick one out."

Mom burst into tears and started thanking the man, but he waved her off and went on his way. She found me and told me we could go buy a bike. She said that I was thrilled but not surprised. "I knew God was going to give me one," she said I had said.

For a long time, that was the full story Mom told. Her little boy wanted a bike, prayed *not my will, but yours be done* prayers for a bike, got a bike. She loved telling that story. When I got serious religion after high school, she told me how she'd held on to that story through my years of teenage backsliding, trusting that I had a gift of faith and would eventually come back to God. When I entered into long periods of spiritual doubt in my twenties (... thirties ... forties ...), she'd tell me that story as a reminder that there was a simpler faith deep down inside me.

"You've always known your heavenly father will provide for you," she said.

I was well into adulthood before Mom filled in the details of this story. How the man who came to the door was the husband of a woman in her Sunday School class. How his wife had come home from church one day and told him that there was a precious young woman at church who'd shared about her son praying for a bicycle and how he prayed for it so sweetly every night. How the story had broken the woman's heart. How she'd told her husband, "You're going to make sure that boy gets a bike." She instructed him to call the church, find out where we lived, and take care of the matter.

Why did it take Mom so long to tell me the full story? Church people always knew the Dodds needed things, and they dropped off clothes and food and small amounts of money. Bike money from a stranger was the most natural thing in the world for me to expect. "I always knew God was going to give me one"—that's how Mom raised me. Maybe she needed it to be a miracle story for her own sake. She was always looking for signs that Father God was taking care of us.

But it mattered to Mom that I understood that when the bikes don't come, God has a hand in that too. He is the God of bikes, and he is the God of bikelessness. The hard work is not believing that God will give you a bike. The hard work is learning to live with disappointment on all the days when all you can do is watch other people ride, even as they sail right over your head.

• • •

In spite of our general acceptance of the idea of God as a father, in the Bible, God is rarely referred to in that way, especially in the oldest stories. It's there, but it's scant—almost as scant as God-as-mother metaphors, which are also there.

Then along comes Jesus, who called God "Father" and encouraged everyone else to do the same: "When you pray, say, 'Our father.'" He described God as a father who understands what his children need even before they ask. He made up parables about families where the fathers are unmistakable representations of God.

One of his most beloved tales is about a wealthy father with two sons. One of the sons leaves home and squanders his inheritance and his morals, then comes back home to his father's loving embrace. It's a beautiful story, and its point is clear: There is a heavenly father who stands ready to receive you. Don't worry about what your brother thinks.

Does the family in that story have a mom? They must have at some point, but she goes unmentioned. Maybe God is like a single dad.

Jesus had a heavenly Father, but on earth his mother was the force of the family. His dad barely registers—Joseph did not sire Jesus, and he did not seem to matter much in his raising. Mary is the one who instructs him, seeks him out, mourns him. She is the one who is present.

So Jesus had a head full of stories about God the father, and he had a life full of stories about his mother. Maybe—to name something that may have occurred to me sooner had I been raised in different Christian soil—his mother was one of the main reasons he was able to get in touch with his heavenly father.

I can relate. My most sustained convictions about God are linked to my mother. The faith I have today is, with a few adaptations, the faith she gave me.

11

Faith Is a Faucet

SOME PEOPLE HAVE faith in God the way Batman and the Punisher have superpowers—built from within through sheer, willful acts of intention. Other people have faith the way Superman and Spider-Man have superpowers—they're born with it, or they acquire it through some freak accident and then they learn to harness it, live with it, and put it to some good use against the challenges of this world.

You don't know how faith comes to the people around you, but you go to church with your fellow believers and you see them singing the songs and taking the bread and wine and praying for their needs and you think, *This whole thing really connects with them.* And you're not looking down on that at all; you're intrigued by it, tempted to it. *However they got here is right on,* you think. *I want what they have.*

But in time, you find that faith is a faucet. It can run gentle, steady, and strong. Hot and cold. It can be turned off, yet still drip. Am I the one turning the knob? Or am I merely the spout?

Faith is a muse that visits, blesses with her presence. How do I make her appear? Not clear, but I have learned that her visits are a blessing. When the muse appears, I sit under her, working, creating, hoping she won't go away. She's a wave I don't pass up; I just ride.

Sometimes a few moments of faith are enough to sustain me for a stretch of faithless road ahead.

I was formed by two distinct American Christian cultures—Southern Baptist until I was eighteen, then a hard pivot to charismatic evangelical for a few intense years. Ultimately, neither expression of faith quite stuck, and for years I looked for ultimate truth in other places. I considered options. For seasons in my twenties and thirties, I figured I was making my way to agnosticism or atheism. But I longed to be one of those quietly confident, intellectually grounded believers. I was haunted by the suspicion that there was something obvious I was missing, something that would make everything click if only I was right-minded. I kept waiting for an experience like the one I had with my sister at seventeen, when she took me on that walk and pointed out the truth that should have been obvious to me all along. *Everyone else gets this*, I said to myself, over and over. *Why don't you?*

I'd lose faith for a stretch. I'd be mired in doubt, no sense of God at all, no way to recognize him in the world despite near-constant efforts to find him. Prayer was a one-way conversation. I thought I was on my way out of the life of faith.

But every now and then, against my expectations, I'd experience a surge of faith—the faucet would come fully on. I'd be running in the woods and find myself talking to God. I'd wake up in the morning and find that I was craving a good, long kneel. I'd talk to someone whose belief in God felt beautiful, clear, nonarbitrary. After many years of these occasional faith surges, I was forced to admit they were not going to go away: The seeds of faith are inside of me. I was not moving toward agnosticism or atheism; I was not moving in a straight line at all. I was moving in circles but not in a closed loop. It was a gentle, upward spiral.

I still pass through great periods of doubt, where I'm ready to believe that nothing is true, that there is no Author and we're alone on a great big space rock. Other times I pass through a deep sense of presence, trusting in a voice that is calling from within and from without. Some days God—the One Who Is Paying Attention—is so obviously present to me that I cannot imagine having doubted.

I feel less in control of all this than I used to; I feel less need to control it.

My faith life bobs and weaves, ebbs and flows. It reminds me of the Guadalupe River a few miles north of my home in Texas. Over my decade living here, I've watched the Guadalupe get down to almost nothing. I've seen it flow so strong that I can get in tubes with my family and float all day along its gentle streams. It's the same river.

One reason it took me so long to settle into this way of being a person of faith is that I was raised by a mother whose faith was strong, clear, unmistakable. I assumed my faith—any faith, really—should work the same way.

Mom believed in God the Father, his son, Jesus Christ, and the Holy Spirit the way you believe that the water will come on at that kitchen faucet every day. It was as basic and reliable as good plumbing. Mom's faith was not a wave; it was the firm ground she stood on. She was highly responsive to the sources of religion all around her—Southern Baptist preachers, Christian devotional books, Christian music, even TV preachers. Never tempted to atheism or agnosticism, the God of the Bible was her God, plain and simple, and reading the Bible turned up the volume of his voice.

Some people wear this kind of faith heavy; some dress it in spikes. Mom wore hers light, like a shawl. You wanted to be under it with her.

12

Mom's Life of Prayer

MOM THANKED GOD for every good thing that happened to her. Surprising things like a new bike for her kid; a just-in-time job; unexpected checks in the mail for food and rent. But also regular things like the sun coming out; the air conditioner kicking on. As we got older, my sister and I mocked her constant God-thanking but only in love and only when Mom was within earshot. We'd open the refrigerator door and say, "Thank you, Jesus." We'd sip a fresh cup of coffee and say, "Hallelujah, Father." We'd turn on the TV to find a favorite *Brady Bunch* rerun and drop to our knees in praise. Mom would giggle with us—a saint, among other things, of laughing at herself.

We were not mocking her actual faith in God, mind you. We rather depended on it.

Mom had various jobs over the years—front desk assistant, office manager, customer service rep. But her primary life's work was prayer. She rose at four or four thirty each morning and got right to it. She'd make coffee and head to the kitchen table, open her Bible and whatever devotional book she was reading, and reach for her Father. When I was a teenager, sometimes I'd come home late at night after a shift at Chick-fil-A or Target. If Mom was sitting at the kitchen table in her pink robe, hair pulled back in a band, Bible splayed open before her, it meant the day with Dad had been particularly hard. Other times I'd come home in the middle of the day to a quiet house, but with Mom's car parked outside, I knew she was home. If I didn't see her in the kitchen or downstairs, I could crack open the door to her bedroom, knowing what I'd find: Mom on her knees at bedside.

She'd read well-worn soft-cover books called *Streams in the Desert* or *My Utmost for His Highest.* Her copies looked like what devotional book publishers must hope for in their most missional dreams: broken spines taped together, pages slipping out, underlinings and marginalia everywhere. She treated those books like clay, shaping them over the years into spiritual artifacts, though for her they were the potter and she was the clay.

And then there was her Bible, which I now keep on my nightstand and leaf through as a way of spending time with her. Filled with marginalia and dates and notes sprawled even on top of the text itself, Mom's Bible is as much journal as Scripture. She treated the text like a two-way conversation. Bible verses spoke out to her from the page, and she spoke back. People sometimes write of *pouring over* the pages of a book when they mean *poring over,* but for Mom the malapropism is apt. She poured herself into Bible pages, midrashing them with her life.

After Mom died in 2018, Kaysie kept the Bible for about a year, hanging onto it while it still carried Mom's smell. Then she let me borrow it, and I've not yet given it back. I will someday, but honestly, this thing belongs in an American religion exhibit at the Smithsonian.

Mom's Life of Prayer

ISAIAH 40:14

Or *as* His counselor has taught Him?
14 With whom did He take counsel, and *who* instructed Him,
And taught Him in the path of justice?
Who taught Him knowledge,
And showed Him the way of understanding?
15 Behold, the nations *are* as a drop in a bucket,
And are counted as the small dust on the scales;
Look, He lifts up the isles as a very little thing.
16 And Lebanon *is* not sufficient to burn,
Nor its beasts sufficient for a burnt offering.
17 All nations before Him *are* as nothing,
And they are counted by Him less than nothing and worthless.

18 To whom then will you liken God?
Or what likeness will you compare to Him?
19 The workman molds an image,
The goldsmith overspreads it with gold,
And the silversmith casts silver chains.
20 Whoever is too impoverished *for such* a contribution
Chooses a tree *that* will not rot;
He seeks for himself a skillful workman
To prepare a carved image *that* will not totter.

21 Have you not known?
Have you not heard?
Has it not been told you from the beginning?
Have you not understood from the foundations of the earth?
22 *It is* He who sits above the circle of the earth,
And its inhabitants are like grasshoppers,
Who stretches out the heavens like a curtain,
And spreads them out like a tent to dwell in.
23 He brings the princes to nothing;
He makes the judges of the earth useless.

24 Scarcely shall they be planted,
Scarcely shall they be sown,
Scarcely shall their stock take root in the earth,
When He will also blow on them,
And they will wither,

And the whirlwind will take them away like stubble.
25 "To whom then will you liken Me,
Or *to whom* shall I be equal?" says the Holy One.
26 Lift up your eyes on high,
And see who has created these things,
Who brings out their host by number;
He calls them all by name,
By the greatness of His might And the strength of *His* power;
Not one is missing.

27 Why do you say, O Jacob,
And speak, O Israel:
"My way is hidden from the LORD,
And my just claim is passed over by my God"?
28 Have you not known?
Have you not heard?
The everlasting God, the LORD,
The Creator of the ends of the earth,
Neither faints nor is weary.
His understanding is unsearchable.
29 He gives power to the weak,
And to *those who have* no might He increases strength.
30 Even the youths shall faint and be weary,
And the young men shall utterly fall,
31 But those who wait on the LORD Shall renew *their* strength;
They shall mount up with wings like eagles,
They shall run and not be weary,
They shall walk and not faint.

41 Israel Assured of God's Help

"Keep silence before Me,
O coastlands,
And let the people renew *their* strength!
Let them come near, then let them speak;
Let us come near together for judgment.

2 "Who raised up one from the east?
Who in righteousness called him to His feet?
Who gave the nations before him,
And made *him* rule over kings?
Who gave *them* as the dust to his sword,
As driven stubble to his bow?
3 Who pursued them, *and* passed safely
By the way *that* he had not gone with his feet?

ISAIAH 41:25

4 Who has performed and done *it*,
Calling the generations from the beginning?
'I, the LORD, am the first;
And with the last I am He.'"
5 The coastlands saw *it* and feared,
The ends of the earth were afraid;
They drew near and came.
6 Everyone helped his neighbor,
And said to his brother,
"Be of good courage!"
7 So the craftsman encouraged the goldsmith;
He who smooths *with* the hammer *inspired* him who strikes the anvil,
Saying, "It is ready for the soldering";
Then he fastened it with pegs,
That it might not totter.

8 "But you, Israel, *are* My servant,
Jacob whom I have chosen,
The descendants of Abraham My friend.
9 You whom I have taken from the ends of the earth,
And called from its farthest regions,
And said to you,
'You *are* My servant,
I have chosen you and have not cast you away:
10 Fear not, for I *am* with you;
Be not dismayed, for I *am* your God.
I will strengthen you,
Yes, I will help you,
I will uphold you with My righteous right hand.'

11 "Behold, all those who were incensed against you
Shall be ashamed and disgraced;
They shall be as nothing,
And those who strive with you shall perish.
12 You shall seek them and not find them—
Those who contended with you.
Those who war against you
Shall be as nothing,
As a nonexistent thing.
13 For I, the LORD your God, will hold your right hand,
Saying to you, 'Fear not, I will help you.'

14 "Fear not, you worm Jacob,
You men of Israel!
I will help you," says the LORD
And your Redeemer, the Holy One of Israel.
15 "Behold, I will make you into a new threshing sledge with sharp teeth;

You shall thresh the mountains and beat them small,
And make the hills like chaff.
16 You shall winnow them, the wind shall carry them away,
And the whirlwind shall scatter them;
You shall rejoice in the LORD,
And glory in the Holy One of Israel.

17 "The poor and needy seek water, but *there is* none,
Their tongues fail for thirst.
I, the LORD, will hear them;
I, the God of Israel, will not forsake them.
18 I will open rivers in desolate heights,
And fountains in the midst of the valleys;
I will make the wilderness a pool of water,
And the dry land springs of water.
19 I will plant in the wilderness the cedar and the acacia tree,
The myrtle and the oil tree;
I will set in the desert the cypress tree *and* the pine
And the box tree together,
20 That they may see and know,
And consider and understand together,
That the hand of the LORD has done this,
And the Holy One of Israel has created it.

21 "Present your case," says the LORD.
"Bring forth your strong *reasons,*" says the King of Jacob.
22 "Let them bring forth and show us what will happen;
Let them show the former things, what they *were,*
That we may consider them,
And know the latter end of them;
Or declare to us things to come.
23 Show the things that are to come hereafter,
That we may know that you *are* gods;
Yes, do good or do evil,
That we may be dismayed and see *it* together.
24 Indeed you *are* nothing,
And your work nothing;
He who chooses you *is* an abomination.

25 "I have raised up one from the north,
And he shall come;
From the rising of the sun he shall call on My name;

Mom's Bible is a record of the people she knew and loved and how she prayed for them. Next to the verses containing what she took as God's promises, Mom wrote the names of her children and, later, her grandchildren. She wrote the names of people I don't recognize, her cousins and coworkers or church friends. Every now and then I see the name of someone Mom knew of only through talking to me, such as David Kuo, a dear friend of mine who died of a brain tumor in 2013. Mom never met David but prayed for him through the many years he struggled against the disease. Tucked deep into the text of this Bible is a folded-up printout of an email exchange between Mom and David detailing their prayers for each other.

Sometimes she scribbled her prayers directly into the text. In the margins of Matthew 9:28—where Jesus has been approached by two blind men asking for healing and he asks them, "Do you believe that I am able to do this?"—Mom wrote, "We do believe you are able!!! So, please heal us—Kaysie, David Kuo, me, and others I am praying for."

Many verses are marked with special occasions. Next to 2 Timothy 1:7, she wrote, "Morgan texted this verse to me before my surgery." All throughout the text, from Genesis to Revelation, dates appear in the margins and next to chapter headings where the Scriptures must have spoken to her in a special way on certain days. The dates start in the late 1970s, when Mom was in her thirties, and continue throughout her adulthood—pretty much my whole life.

Sometimes a Psalm number will be circled with a particular date scribbled next to it. Psalm 37 says "9/11/82." Psalm 40 says "Aug. 2010." Sometimes a date just appears in the margin, Mom marking the day that verse struck her in a special way: "3/13/06—FOR ME" it says next to Psalm 37:34 and "Aug 1979" next to Psalm 40:1. Many verses are dated in a faded color and then again in another, bold color, as she marked her scriptural returns over the years.

Mom also wrote affirmations to herself throughout the Bible: "Be joyful in the Lord!"; "I trust you, Lord!" She transcribed key points of sermons she was listening to. She wrote quick summaries of the Bible teaching she'd heard from a million preachers over a million hours of listening to sermons.

More than anything else, she wrote praise. "Thank you, Father God!" is scattered throughout the text.

Some books of Mom's Bible contain almost as much text from her as they do from, well, whoever wrote that part of the Bible. The short New Testament epistle of Philippians is an explosion of ink—blue, red, black—showing how she returned to those four chapters again and again. In the narrow space between the opening verses, where Paul tells "the saints in Philippi" that he's praying for their "love to abound still more and more in knowledge and discernment," Mom wrote her own name, Dawn. Mom was always telling me to insert my name into Scriptures to remind myself that they are written to me too. Where Paul tells his audience that he wants them to be "filled with the fruits of righteousness," she wrote, "Fill me, dear God!" Other verses have big arrows coming out of them, pointing to "For me!" and "Always for me!" in the margins. I'm straight-up regaling her here, but I confess that if this were some stranger's Bible, I'd likely see these markings in a different light. They'd strike me as a sentimental, problematic expression of individualistic Christianity. This text is ancient. It comes from a time and a place and a people most of us can barely imagine. And pretty much the whole thing, from Genesis to Revelation, is a communal text, written with whole communities of people in mind. Rigorous theological debates have raged for centuries about who those communities were and what these scriptural stories meant to them, and perhaps it's not for some modern white American woman to reduce them to *For me!*

Be that as it may, I also have the evidence of Mom's life. I know what her devotional practice actually did for Mom day in, day out. I know what it did for those around her.

Deep prayer lives can make people weird or dour or hard to talk to. But Mom's made her into a well-regulated person. It made her joyful in the face of everyday deprivation, betrayal, and fear. Prayer made her who she needed to be to face the day.

Mom is famous among those who knew her. Maybe several hundred people total had the chance over the course of her lifetime, and around two hundred or so of those crowded into a northeastern Mississippi funeral home on the day of her memorial service in late February 2018. If you were there, you were a Dawn enthusiast, because anyone lucky enough to know her became enthusiastic about her. That's in part because her own enthusiasm—for peanut butter crackers, for popcorn cooked on the stovetop, for your description of what you'd cooked the night before, for drinking out of Mason jars, for walking at the fastest clip, for the sound of a bird in the backyard, for the smell of the lotion she'd just gotten from Walgreens, for the peel of clouds in the sky, for any kind of change in weather, for the joke someone just told, for the movie she'd just watched, for the new shirt you were wearing, for the trip you were about to take or the one you'd just come back from, and okay, for whatever you were saying to her at anytime you were saying it—was infectious.

Mom was the best mood lighting in every room. But she would not set the mood so much as match it, then warm it.

She'd fill your ears with her sayings. "Polly Wolly!" when the air was too cold or too hot. "I'm caving in!" when she was hungry. "This old knockabout?" in response to you saying her dress looked nice that day. "My law!" or "My land!" interchangeably as her version of "Holy shit!" Every little kid was "the sweetest thing" and everything they said was "I do believe, the sweetest thing I have ever heard." When she came for a visit, you'd find yourself adopting her language, as if saying what she said would help you be what she was.

On the day of her funeral, I got a long text from a friend I'd seen only a handful of times over the previous twenty years. He told me he'd never felt close to his own mom, but he'd always remembered a time when we were in college and he came over to watch a movie with me when we were both home on break. At some point, Mom entered the room, sat down next to him on the couch, and put her arm around him. "I'm so glad you're here," she said and snuggled with him for a long moment.

"I doubt she'd even remember that," he texted. "It's just who she was in her everyday life. But I still think about it twenty years later. It defined for me how I want my own kids to feel around me."

Mom's way left a mark. She fashioned for us a way of being soft in a hard world. She straightened our crooked path.

And after watching her be who she was for more than forty years, and after spending hours thumbing through her Bible, I know how she did it. She built herself from within every single day. She woke up, and she focused.

I think about her when I wake up every morning, trying to decide how long I can go before I check my phone. Once I do, there are new emails and NBA scores and WhatsApp threads and news headlines and leftover SMS notifications. I've cut social media out of my life almost entirely and managed to reduce the noise by only a fraction. Once I break the seal on my phone, I'm thinking about the things I need to do when I leave the house today and the things I left undone yesterday. I'm thinking about what one of my kids is going through or a sticky situation with a colleague or something my wife and I still need to talk about. I wake up to a churning mind.

I've tried all sorts of remedies for quietude. I've stepped outside as soon as I wake up. I've sat on the couch for meditation. Right now my strategy is to begin my day by moving my body. I make the coffee, feed the dog, and then start foam rolling and stretching and cat-cowing and planking and bird dogging and push-upping and rolling the soles of my feet. This approach is helpful on some days—after fifteen or twenty minutes of moving my body in the predawn, my mind settles into the silence that was there all along, just waiting for me.

What I find in that silence is, I believe, something like what Mom found. I'm nervous to type it out, because I've always had a hard time believing that it is true. But what I find is God.

My wont has been to hold onto my doubt and my skepticism, a natty blanket always within reach. But when I let it all go, when I take a chance, I confess that Mom was on to something. She spent years trying to give me the gift of faith. On my best days, I receive it.

• • •

Mom was herself—the person she built through her daily work of prayer—until the bitter end, when breast cancer took her life after a decade-long battle. In the face of all the weight and hair loss and endless hours in hospital gowns and all the rest, she kept choosing faith and hope. She kept choosing the possibility of life. In her last few days in the hospital, the doctor sat at her bedside and said they'd done all they could do.

Best case scenario, she had a few months to live. Probable case, a few weeks. It was time, he said, to talk about hospice.

"Well, that's your report," she told him. "I believe God's report."

Maybe when you read those words on this page, they sound stern, Christian curt. They sound like someone neglecting the *not my will, but yours be done* rule of prayer. But I was there when she said them, and I swear to you they were winsome and sweet, as if she were noting the afternoon sun parting rain clouds.

The doctor smiled down upon her. "I know you do," he said. "I like that about you."

13

Father in Heaven, Mother on Earth

UP UNTIL SEVENTH or eighth grade, I had church friends and school friends, and never the twain shall meet. Mom always encouraged the church friendships and worried over the school friendships. She'd rather drive me across town to spend a Saturday afternoon with a church friend than let me walk a couple of blocks over to a school friend's house. Her worry was pointed in the wrong direction—Southern Baptist youth-group friends were the source of my first cigarettes, my first booze, my first few times feeling up and being felt up.

Our family's church attendance wavered during middle school, then dropped off completely during high school. Kaysie was off at college, two states over, and apparently, she'd been the driver of our churchgoing. Mom kept attending here and there, but she didn't force the issue with me. Dad was glad to stay home and get his Sunday tipple going, and I was glad to stay home with comic books and *Sports Illustrated*.

I'm told by old high school pals that I was a voluble believer in those days, eager to talk about God and sin and death and the afterlife. I have no memory of being that way.

Our school had an evangelical clique and a Catholic clique, and I was not part of either. But they tell me I spoke of heaven and hell and the existence of angels, especially on the nights we drank and smoked weed and had no girls around. I'll take my buddies' word for it. Mostly, I just remember how lousy I felt about all the drinking and the smoking and the girls. I was a guilt-ridden teenage partier.

Starting when I was sixteen, around the time Kaysie moved back into the house and we had that eye-opening conversation about Dad's drinking, I spiraled for a year or so. Stacie's party was one of many such nights where I pushed myself to the edge of danger, and one thing my high school pals and I agree on is that we're lucky we survived. One night while driving around with a bunch of friends, I passed out behind the wheel of the car, and we coasted into a lucky stop. Another night—again, behind the wheel of a car but this time after smoking weed laced with cocaine—I hallucinated that my legs had turned to water, and I grabbed a pen and started stabbing them to make them solid again. One night, I climbed onto a stack of railroad ties outside a friend's apartment, blacked out, and face-planted from several feet straight onto the concrete slab below. I woke up with a chipped front tooth and my face torn apart from my forehead down to my chin—my upper lip still bears a scar.

With my friends, I pretended that these episodes were hilarious. But when I lay in bed alone at night, I was terrified of who and what I was becoming. I was becoming my father, or something worse.

Not that he noticed. It was easy to hide things from Dad, preoccupied as he was with his own drinking regimen. So long as I cleaned the garage and mowed the lawn according to his specifications, I could more or less do as I pleased.

But Mom was paying attention. I don't mean she was monitoring my bad behavior—paying attention was her way of life. She was always present, tuned in. She stayed on top of who my friends were and how they were doing, what condition my clothes were in and when we were going to need to figure out how to replace this or that. She was there when I woke up in the morning. She waited for me to come home from work at night. She asked gentle questions about my day. And I would tell her a lot. We were pals.

She definitely knew I was up to no good. She confronted me about it from time to time. She'd ask if I was drinking, doing drugs, tell me what she could smell on my clothes. She led with concern, not accusation or nagging. She was checking in. She was loving her wayward son.

And then I would commit a sin worse than any other: I would lie to my mom. I would encourage her to trust me. I built up an entire fantasy world for her, one where I was always working late at Chick-fil-A or Target and being there for friends who needed me and designated driving. Or I was spending long weekends helping my friends' parents with projects at their houses. I got other people involved in the lie—my pals became experts at talking to my mom about the very good boys that we were. Once I even persuaded a friend's mom to call my mom and tell her that she'd invited me to some kind of family event. Would it be okay if I stayed with them overnight? We smoked joints with my friend's parents that night and laughed about how we could get my mom to believe anything.

I was toying with the most important relationship in my life. I was robbing myself of it. And while I worried from time to time about the fires of hell in those years, the more pressing concern was that Mom was going to find out who her son really was—and that the truth about me would crush her.

• • •

It was midway through my senior year of high school when I started going back to church with my sister. Kaysie was wise to my bad behavior, and she kept inviting me to come to church services with her. She was direct: "You need God back in your life." I obliged her here and there. I remember sitting in a worship service hoping she didn't know I was hungover, and in another worship service hoping she didn't know I was high.

But I went, and I listened, and after a while I felt that I was just postponing the inevitable: Kaysie was right. The way I was living was temporary, doomed to fail. I needed to get my life right. Plus, I remembered exactly what Mom would have wanted me to remember. I was still the kid who prayed the *not my will, but yours be done* prayers. I longed to be back in God's good graces. I longed to know that God was pleased with me. And I longed to be able to reconnect with my mother.

I let a few altar calls come and go. But one Sunday morning, as I rode shotgun in Kaysie's car on the way to church, I decided that when the altar call happened that day, I was going to respond. I would leave my seat and go *rededicate my life to Christ*. And then something occurred to me: If I got right with God, I would get a big bonus. I could reconnect with Mom, reestablishing trust and honesty between us.

I did go forward to the altar that day, and I did immediately go home and try to make things right with Mom. But it took several months to reset my life—to peel away from the parties, to stop smoking so much weed, to get curious enough about the Bible to actually open it. The altar call conversion part happened quickly. The actual rededication took most of the next year.

As I've said, in the first year after high school, I stayed home and went to the local college, the University of Colorado-Colorado Springs, which was at the time just a commuter school. Being home that year helped me commit to my new Christian lifestyle. Most of my high school friends were gone, and while I'd relapse for a few nights of partying whenever they came home for a visit, mostly I built a new life with new church friends. My church involvement snowballed—two services each Sunday morning, Sunday afternoon volleyball with church friends, Sunday night services, Tuesday prayer services, Friday night college ministry.

Kaysie had moved out of the house again, so our home was back to Mom, Dad, and me, which really meant Mom and me. Dad was there in body but otherwise not—he ate, drank, slept. He was like a stench that you cannot quite find the source of, can't quite cleanse away.

But Mom and I engaged. Now that I was home more and stabilizing, we really lived in that house together, settling into a rhythm of meals and housework, long walks and old movies. The more involved I got at church, the more intense about my faith, the deeper my relationship with her could go. We connected around the prayers we prayed each day. We connected around the parts of the Bible we were reading. We shared Bible verses with each other, trading insights and inspirations. We started reading the same devotional books, checking in with each other about the daily passages. I dove deep into Christian music, pushing my favorite artists—Jars of Clay, Rich Mullins, Keith Green, Pray for Rain—onto Mom. "I really love the message," she'd say, a sure sign that she did not like the music, but no matter. We were relating. Our friendship was growing.

And so was our partnership around the biggest challenge in our lives: dealing with Dad. We related over our broken hearts, our hopes for Dad, our belief that God the Father wanted to save my earthly father. We read books and listened to audio cassette tapes about healing prayer and spiritual warfare, learning techniques that might make our prayers more effectual. Once, upon the advice of one of our books, we spent a couple of hours praying over each room in our home, "loosing the spirit of God" and asking for "the cleansing blood of Jesus" to cover every inch of the home. We committed to days of fasting together. We begged God to release Dad from his torment, to exorcise the demons of addiction that held sway in our home. Sometimes we admitted to each other that we did not know if any of this was the right thing to do, but prayer like this was cooked spaghetti we could throw on the wall. Why not try? Why not bang the doors of heaven? We had nothing to lose.

I picked up a job at a local ice cream shop, and I'd get home from work late at night. Invariably, Mom would be sitting at the kitchen table, waiting for me with our favorite snack—stovetop popcorn, slices of cheddar cheese, orange juice. We'd eat and talk about the Bible passages we'd read that day. We'd talk about how dad was doing. Sometimes he'd be passed out on the couch, one room over. Sometimes he'd be out of the house, not yet back from his own job teaching night school an hour away in Pueblo. We'd pray together, asking God to intervene, to heal him, to do a miracle in our lives.

One night as we sat and talked and prayed, we heard the automatic garage door open and Dad's car pulling in. A moment later, the door into the kitchen opened, and Dad stumbled through it and right onto the kitchen floor. He was so drunk he couldn't stand, couldn't speak, could hardly move. How had he made it home alive? How had he not killed anyone on his way? Mom crumpled down next to him, sobbing,

"Oh, Bill! Oh, Bill!" I pulled him up, draped him across my back, and carried him upstairs to the bathroom. I dropped him into the tub and told him to stay there until he sobered up. I went back downstairs and told Mom we needed to get out of the house. We walked around the neighborhood for an hour, talking and praying and asking God when, when, when any of this would ever change.

Nothing we tried worked. Mom stayed with Dad for much longer than she should have, and I prayed believing he would change for much longer than I should have. He was never going to change. But I could not be made to see that, and neither could Mom. It would be some years before either of us would engage other versions of counseling that suggested other kinds of interventions—necessary boundaries, orienting around the internal work we needed to do on ourselves, not just the work we wanted the Lord to do in him.

I did hear some good advice from one of the megachurch pastors I so admired in those days. I just was not able to receive his wisdom. I'd set up a lunch with him at Chili's for the sole purpose of talking about my dad. I told Kaysie and Mom excitedly of my plans, how I was going to share with him both some details of Dad's behavior and talk about our faith that God could do a miracle. I wanted to know how he thought we should be praying, how to intercede most powerfully. I felt sure he'd point me to a spiritual solution that could turn things around. I played up my faith, assuring him that I really did believe God could heal my dad. I tried to impress him with my trust in God's power to make everything okay.

When I was done, the pastor looked at me squarely.

"Look," he said. "I do believe God can heal your dad of his addictions. But you need to understand something: It might not happen. Your dad may be an alcoholic until he dies."

He let that sink in for a moment, then continued. "The most important question is not whether God is going to heal your dad. The most important question is whether you are going to be okay even if your dad drinks every day for the rest of his life."

I went home and told Mom what the pastor had said. We sat there together in silence, absorbing the blow. We wanted to believe God's report could mean only one thing: Dad would be healed. We wanted to leave out the *not my will, but yours be done* part.

14

The Years the Locusts Ate

MOM BELIEVED IN God for many things. Material things—debts cleared, groceries to fill the pantry, new shoes and jackets just in time for the school year. Abstract things—that he was present, he loved her, and he was watching over her children and grandchildren. However dire our straits, Mom chose to believe that better days were coming. "We are hard-pressed on every side, yet not crushed," it says in 2 Corinthians 4:8–9, a passage she marked on repeat over the years with underlines and circles and check marks, plus one red ink smudge bearing the mark of a teardrop. "We are perplexed, yet not in despair; persecuted, but not forsaken; struck down, but not destroyed."

The older I got, the more I pressed her on this belief. How do you know? What makes you think that's even possible, given all you've gone through? How much longer do we need to put up with this man in our lives?

"The Lord will return to me the years that the locusts have eaten," she told me.

She got the phrase from the last few verses of Joel 2. It comes at the close of a fever-pitched passage of prophecy describing a dreadful, backbreaking "day of the Lord"—heaven and earth trembling, God's army consuming the land. But all of a sudden, as if in a fit of holy whimsy, the Lord's vengeance flips to mercy: "Who knows? He may turn and relent and leave behind a blessing." Israel repents with all their hearts, and the winter turns to spring—rain falls, pastures spring up, fruit trees bend with bounty. God clears his own debts with his chosen people: "I will repay you for the years the locusts have eaten . . . my great army that I sent among you."

The passage contains a terrible recognition: The locusts are from God too. So what can you do to make the locusts go away? Is repentance the only available pesticide? And what if you've already been repenting for some time? Can you make a move? Or can you only wait on the Lord to move things for you? How do you know when he is going to turn and relent?

In Mom's Bible, Joel 2 bursts with the ink of several pens—red, black, blue, purple. The marks span decades, as early as 1979 and running through 2017. The margins around the passage bear lengthy notes: "God gave this promise to me many years ago—and recently," says one. "Thank you, Father God! You have dealt wondrously with me all my life!" says another.

Two of the specific dates in these margins are familiar to me.

January 2007—she must have marked it on the morning she finally found the resolution she'd long been looking for.

In early February of that year, Mom called her brother, Mike, asked him to come pick her up, and left my dad for good.

April 2010—with bright red ink, Mom marked the month her second marriage began, the date Mom believed God's report had finally come to pass. "Mine and Jack's wedding day!" she wrote. "Praise God!"

• • •

Some backstory is in order here. Kaysie Dawn Deaton—my mom, who went by Dawn—was born the second of four kids in mid-century Belmont, Mississippi, a one-stoplight town in the northeastern corner of the state. When she was five years old, her dad drowned while fishing in a nearby lake. Her mom was left to raise four kids ages six and under: Karen, Dawn, Mike, and baby Beth. The Deatons grew up hard and poor—dinners of cornbread and milk, winters of a house that couldn't get warm, summers and falls of working the cotton fields. They also grew up thick as thieves, surrounded by grandparents and uncles and aunts and cousins and close friends. Fatherless but family-rich, Dawn had a childhood she cherished, and she never expected or wanted to venture very far from Belmont.

She also had young love: a junior high and high school sweetheart named Jack. Like teenagers sometimes do, Dawn and Jack pledged to be together forever. I grew up knowing Jack's name but not because she told me about him. In her near-daily phone calls with her sister Karen, who still lived in Mississippi, every now and then I'd overhear her asking for updates on a guy I first assumed was a beloved cousin. "Heard anything from Jackie lately?" "Did you hear that Susan ran into Jackie?"

Jack was a year older than Dawn. When he graduated from Belmont High School in 1966, he headed two hours south to Starkville to attend MSU. Dawn planned to follow him there one year later, and so she did. But when she got there, she found that Jack had embraced campus life. He was a fraternity brother, and he was having a grand old time about it. When Dawn and Jack were one-on-one, he was still sweet on her, but in social settings he changed. He wouldn't hold her hand in public or put his arm around her. She noticed he was friendly with other girls.

Dawn didn't say much about it all through her first year, but as the spring semester came to a close, she decided to confront Jack.

"I thought we were going to be together," she told him. "I thought you wanted to build a life with me."

"I do want that," he said. "We are going to be together. But first, I want to be free to enjoy my college years."

"That's not good enough for me," she told him. They broke up.

Dawn decided that a long summer in the tiny town of Belmont, where she might see Jack around any corner, was not what she needed. When the semester was over, she went home for a brief visit, then moved back to Starkville for summer school.

That's when she met Bill Dodd.

She knew who Bill was already, as he had been dating her roommate, Peggy. But she hadn't paid him any mind. Turns out Peggy was just a path to Dawn—he'd dumped Peggy, and now Bill wanted to know if Dawn would go out sometime. She declined. He was twenty-six and a college dropout, but he still hung around the campus a lot. She wasn't sure what he was all about.

But Bill was persistent, and Dawn was brokenhearted. Why not let him take her out? He made her a no-pressure offer—he was meeting up with a group of friends, and he'd love to bring her along. Just a hangout with some nice people. She said yes.

Bill picked up Dawn in a yellow convertible, dressed to the nines. He was "making money hand over fist," or so Dawn soon told Karen. That's why he'd dropped out of college years ago; he was making so much cash selling insurance that it didn't make sense to get a diploma. But he stuck around school because everybody wanted him around. He'd been the head cheerleader at MSU and really active in a fraternity that threw legendary parties—Johnny Cash had come to one! Bill even had a nickname: Toddy Doddy. She wasn't sure what that meant.

Had he mentioned that he was leading a local Bible study? He said God was calling him to be a preacher.

For the next few weeks, Bill showered Dawn with attention. He paid for everything. He opened doors for her. He made public declarations of his affection, putting his arm around her and holding her hand in front of everyone. He talked of setting up a life of plenty through selling insurance and a life of changing the world through preaching.

One afternoon, Bill was with Dawn when she was opening her mail. One of the letters was from the United States Department of Education, confirmation of the federal student aid grant she would be receiving for the upcoming school year. It spelled out how much of the funds would be going to MSU to cover tuition and room and board and how much she'd be receiving as a dividend to cover other expenses.

He pointed at the dividend figure. "They're sending you that money?" he asked.

She nodded. "I'll have it in August. It's how I'll pay for things this fall."

Soon after, Bill surprised Dawn with an engagement ring. It had a big diamond, one made affordable by the presence of a significant flaw. But at the moment, Dawn didn't have an eye for flaws.

Bill said they should get married and they should do so right away. Dawn wasn't so sure. But Bill pressed. She recounted the evidence in her mind—his public affection, his popularity, his financial security, his call to preach. She decided she could trust him.

A few weeks after Dawn and Bill's first date, they became husband and wife.

I once asked my mother when she first knew she'd made a mistake in marrying Dad. "On my honeymoon," she said, then told me a sad story about how they ran out of money on their four-day trip to Chattanooga. They were window-shopping and she asked him "for some little doohickey" to remember their trip by. "I ain't got no money for things like that!" he snapped. He did have enough money to bring beer back to their hotel room, but when it was time to go home, he had to call his mom to wire funds for gas to get back home and groceries for Dawn to cook.

Not long ago, my aunt Beth told me a different story. Dawn told Beth that even as she was walking down the aisle on the day of her wedding, she was whispering to herself, "Come on, Jackie. Don't let me do this. Sneak in through that back door and come get me."

• • •

I used to reason that if Dawn Deaton made a mistake in marrying Bill Dodd, maybe my own life is a mistake. But I do not believe that is true. I do not believe my sister and I, nor the grandchildren of Bill and Dawn Dodd, all exist as the result of a mistake. On some level, every human is a cosmic accident; but once we're here, we're not accidental. We're unmistakable.

Sure, nineteen-year-old Dawn rushed into marriage. Bill got a lucky rebound, and he shined just bright enough to blind her to his faults long enough to seal the deal. At the time, he probably thought he loved her enough to become a better man. She probably thought she loved him back. They were young and passionate and dumb, and they leapt into a life-altering decision. It's a tale as old as time.

Perhaps Mom's mistake came later, when she stayed with Dad all those years in the face of all the evidence that she should have left. Lord knows she had plenty of reasons to leave and even plenty of opportunity. Dad's own family members tried to persuade her to leave him not too long after they first got married and for years ongoing. Me-Me tells me that not long after she met Mom, she told her Billy had never been any good, was never going to be any good, and she should just get out. When Dad decided to move us to California in the mid-1980s, Me-Me confronted Mom about it: "You have no business letting him move you and those kids across the country." But Mom couldn't see it Me-Me's way. She felt she had to stick it through.

Mom's brother and sisters worked her over on the issue even more, trying to help her see exit ramps for years on end. "Fake and phony" was their shorthand description for their brother-in-law. They brainstormed plans with her, pointed out places she could stay, offered solutions for helping raise Kaysie and me. Mom once took us to Tupelo, sans Dad, for a couple of weeks to stay with her sister Karen. Dad called every day of those two weeks to say he couldn't live without her. Another couple of times, she took us to stay with her brother, Mike. Those trips were soft ultimatums to my father, trying to prove that she was willing to leave him. Her siblings pestered her to make the commitment firm. *Don't go back! Just tell Bill it is over. Don't put up with him one minute more.* Each time, Mom would get on the phone with Dad, and Dad would persuade her that, this time, he could change, but only if she helped him.

So she stayed. She kept staying. Karen believes that the decision to stay was not even something Mom wrestled with all that much once a few of those early years had passed. "She was resolved to the fact that she had had her chance to go," Karen told me. "And this was now what she had to do."

Mom and Dad together was the working assumption of our home. It took me years to question her commitment to him. Their being together was as basic as the sun rising every day. Even as I became an adult and got really clear on Dad's addictions and deceptions and utter unreliability, it did not occur to me for a long time that leaving him was a live option for her.

I've celebrated Mom's faith here, but arguably her decision to stay with Dad shows the shadow side of her religious devotion. The Bible, of course, has a few famous/infamous passages that speak to the issue of divorce, and they can be tough reading for people in troubled marriages. For example, 1 Corinthians 7:39 says, "A woman is bound to her husband as long as he lives." In Mark 10:9, when asked about divorce, Jesus replies, "What God has joined together, let no one separate." A moment later, he adds, "If [a woman] divorces her husband and marries another, she commits adultery." Then there are passages like Peter 3:1, which has this to say to women who may be, in biblical parlance, unequally yoked: "Wives, in the same way submit yourselves to your own husbands so that, if any of them do not believe the word, they may be won over without words by the behavior of their wives, when they see the purity and reverence of your lives."

I asked Mom about these passages a couple of times, and she did not have all that much to say about them beyond "Yes, I know." And I can see now that these passages in Mom's Bible are notably free of her own ink. The texts around them bear plenty of her underlinings and marginalia, but the divorce texts? The passages on marriage? Clean as the day they were printed. No dates marked. No "For me!"

But I don't believe the Bible was the handcuffs on Mom. My guess is that, at best, these verses provided a kind of cold comfort. They assured her of the righteousness of the thing she'd already decided to do.

• • •

In 2006, after most of a lifetime of staying with Dad, after Kaysie and I were long gone and raising families of our own, after all of us had more or less stopped wondering if she was ever going to leave, Mom took a trip to Mississippi for a family reunion. She'd not been back in ages. At the time, she and Dad were living in a small apartment in Tulsa, a few miles from my sister and her family. Dad's drinking and health were reaching new lows. I remember feeling so excited for Mom to get some time away from him but worrying that going back to the Deep South would just remind her how heartbroken she was to have been taken from it all those years ago.

The day after Mom got back from the reunion, she called me at my home in Colorado and asked if I would send her a copy of *My Faith So Far*, my memoir of religious conversion and confusion that had come out a couple of years before. "I saw an old friend, and he wants to read it," she said.

We'd never talked about Jack before, but something about the sound of her voice made everything clear to me.

"Is that old friend named Jackie?" I asked.

"Yes, son," she said. "I saw Jackie."

Jack had stayed all those years in the Deep South, mostly in Florence, Alabama, just an hour northeast of Belmont. He had raised two kids and retired from a career as a teacher. He was a widower, having lost his wife to cancer a decade before.

"Wow, Mom. That's amazing that you saw him. Are y'all going to stay in touch?"

"I think so. It was nice to see him. I think we'll be friends."

Within a few months, it was clear that Mom never really came back from that trip to the family reunion. Some combination of seeing Jack and just being back home among all her family and friends inspired Mom to do the thing that she had not been able to do for almost forty years. It took her most of the next year, but little by little she gave herself permission to imagine moving on.

Who knows? He may turn and relent and leave behind a blessing.

Uncle Mike tells me that throughout the decades of Mom and Dad's marriage, his phone calls with his sister often ended the same way: "Let me know when you want me to come get you. Just say the word and I'm on my way." In February 2007, Mom called Mike in Mississippi and told him she was ready. He picked her up the next day.

Dad had lied about many things over the years, but when he told Mom that he would die without her, he was not kidding. With Mom gone, the only sustenance Dad took in was booze. With me living seven hundred miles away, Kaysie was left to care for Dad—at great cost to herself—through the rest of that agonizing year. He died less than ten months after Mom left. We gathered in Tulsa to clean out his apartment and go through the motions of a memorial, then Mom went back to Mississippi.

15

The Addiction Expert

MOM'S BIBLE HAS a frontispiece where you are meant to mark how and when the Bible came into your life. It says, "This Holy Bible Presented to _____ By _____" and then has another blank line for the date. Mom filled this out, noting it as given to "Dawn Dodd" by "My friend and co-worker [whose name I can't make out]" on "September 2006." It was given to her around the same time she went to that family reunion, around the same time she reconnected with Jack.

I only recently noticed this frontispiece. For years, I thought the Bible was the same one I'd seen with her all throughout my childhood. The dates she sprinkled throughout the text encouraged that belief, and they are highly specific—lots of months and years but also many individual days, such as "6/3/1979."

But now I can see that Mom was marking her memories. She'd read a verse, and it would take her back into the long ago. She'd know exactly what had happened on particular days decades past. This Bible is a contemporaneous record of her prayers, her hopes, and her faith. But it is also a memory box of her suffering.

The Lord returned to Mom the years the locusts had eaten. But he returned only a few.

Within the first two years of receiving this Bible, a lot would change for Mom. She would leave Dad and he would die without her, just as he always told her he would. She would move back to Mississippi and into the arms of family and old friends. She would begin to explore new love, or actually renewed love, as she and Jack began dating and imagining a long late life together.

She would begin to engage Jack in particular around one of his children, a son named Carter, who was in his late twenties when Mom and Jack reconnected. Carter was addicted to opioids, trapped in a long cycle of rehab and relapse. As Mom told Kaysie and me about her attempts to assist and intervene, we worried for her greatly. She'd just spent forty years hemmed in by an addict. Was this really a wise move for her? But Mom felt she had a lifetime of lessons to offer—and anyway, no one was going to talk her out of building a life with the man she loved.

Just as all this was unfolding, Mom was diagnosed with breast cancer. When she called to tell me this, I treated it—in my heart and head—like she was telling me she had the flu. It would suck, but she'd get through it. It could not be otherwise, because the locust years had just begun to be returned—no, the return hadn't even really started. We were all still recovering, still living with all that had happened. As glad as I was that Mom had finally left Dad, his last year was torture—especially for Kaysie, into whose arms fell all of Dad's care as he spiraled toward death. We were processing the pains of that year, and we were also adjusting to life as a family spread thin across many miles of this big country, no roots anywhere. Kaysie and I were supporting Mom in her resettlement "back home" while waking to the reality that just as she finally got free, the parent who had always been our rock, our source, was now going to have to be shared with a new family, a new life in her old home.

And now, breast cancer, stage four, prognosis uncertain.

Jack had nursed his first wife through her own sickness, and he knew what he was doing. He invited Mom to live with him while she underwent radiation and chemotherapy, then a double mastectomy followed by more medicine. Kaysie and I watched from afar, visiting her in northern Alabama as we were able. I hoped that God would remember that his promise was to return the years the locusts had eaten, not bring new locusts.

The surgery and medicines worked, and for a while the cancer was held at bay. Mom and Jack married in April 2010. We had not been able to find a time that would make the ceremony work for all our families, or a way to make it affordable, so we celebrated them from our respective homes. In the months after Mom and Jack's marriage, they visited Kaysie and her family in Tulsa and my family and me in Colorado.

Mom and I stayed up late one night over the course of their visit and she told me many of the stories that appear in the pages of this book. She also told me that she was sure that cancer was a minor setback compared to God's promise to her. He was finally doing it—he was returning to her the years that the locusts had eaten.

She was back in her beloved Deep South, living with Jack in Florence, within a stone's throw of Belmont, Mississippi. Her three siblings lived in different towns but within easy driving distance of each other. Cousins and nieces and nephews and childhood friends were all nearby. She kept working as much as her health would allow, and without Dad taking and wasting all the money, she had the financial means to visit her children and grandchildren a couple of times a year. She and Jack got involved in a local church, just as she'd always wanted to do, and she became a dedicated volunteer in the church's poverty ministry. She worked in "Jack's garden," which she called it for a long time before finally converting to "our garden."

Mom had ten years with Jack, and they were as good as ten years can be when you're on radiation and chemotherapy every other year. Every day that she was not sick was a good day because she made it that way. You can go to Florence and have dinner with the people from her church and Carter and his wife, Hannah, and the woman who worked at the farmers' market and the doctors and nurses who worked in her wing at the hospital. Ask them about her. They will remember her. She was the praying woman, the woman who dressed in pink and spoke blessings over everyone who came into her room. "We will be talking about her for a long time," one of the nurses told me on the last day Mom was in the hospital. I believe it.

Mom's memorial service in Belmont, Mississippi, was standing room only. Kaysie and I stood for eons receiving people, many of them saying some version of the same thing: *She was my best friend.*

All the same, when she died, I felt God had some explaining to do. What kind of return on locust years was this? What kind of God allows (or brings!) a pestilence, then promises to make it right, and then makes it right in such a chintzy way? A decade with Jack, half that decade filled with sickness, after four decades of putting up with Bill Dodd? No one deserves that, least of all this woman who mothered and fathered me and friended so many other people.

Hey God, is this the way you're going to return the years the locusts have eaten? Maybe just keep them.

• • •

Or maybe something else is going on.

Last spring while driving through Florida, Mississippi, and Tennessee to learn whatever I could about my father, I took a detour one evening to Florence. I'd arranged to have dinner with Mom's second family—Jack, Carter, and Hannah, along with their two young kids, a toddler girl and a baby boy. We had not seen each other for five years, since Mom's death in February 2018.

I love these people, and I also *like* them—I enjoy their company. They'd been close to Mom, and she'd shared a lot of life with them during her years married to Jack. Hannah and Mom were, as Mom would say, "peas in a pod," and they shared meals and makeup ideas and clothing ideas and talked about anything and everything. Carter and Mom had gone deep into each other's lives, especially around the topics of addiction and recovery. Kaysie and I had also spent a lot of time with Jack, Carter, and Hannah in the last few months of Mom's life when she was in and out of the hospital and then on hospice. We'd all gone through something hard together. We're not in touch much now, but there's a closeness that comes through shared love and shared grief.

For that very reason, as I covered the miles to Florence, I was filled with dread.

Like me, they love Mom. They'd want to talk about her, and that meant I'd have to think about her. It meant I'd have to remember her. I adore my mom, as these pages have shown, but it has taken me many months to write these pages because the act of remembering her is so painful. Grief, like faith, is something best embraced as a practice. I'm just not very good at practicing either—I would rather wait for them to catch me by surprise.

Jack had graciously invited me to spend the night at his house, which was the last place I saw Mom. In the weeks

Mom was on home hospice, Kaysie, Jack, and I took turns sitting by the hospital bed that had been carted into Jack's living room. The three of us gathered there together over her body as she expired. Jack's living room is the site of one of the most painful moments of my life, and to stay with him I had to go back there, be in that space, sit in that awful memory. I was grateful for the invitation, and I wanted time with Jack, but as I drove into town, I was tempted to pull over and open the HotelTonight app.

We met for dinner at a lively, crowded Italian grill called Ricatoni's, which was one of Mom's favorite restaurants. I cannot hear the name Ricatoni except in her voice. It was so good to see everyone, and within moments we were pleasantly catching up. I remembered not just her, but how much I love her people. They are connected to my mom, but they are also living their own good and admirable lives—Jack as an engaged father and grandfather; Hannah as a committed schoolteacher and mom; Carter as an expert copy and print technician and dad—and I'm glad to know they exist in this world.

Carter had recently gotten his eleven-year sobriety coin. He looked great, and he *is* great. He's alert, driven, grounded in the good life he is building. Carter will always stand for me as a testament to recovery. Sobriety is possible (it really is something people can do) and Carter has been walking that walk for over a decade now. The printer company Carter works for is owned by a man who is also in recovery, and Carter had recently turned down another job in part just to stay in this man's orbit. Carter has become something of a force in the recovery world in northern Alabama—he travels around, making appearances at various recovery meetings and sharing his story.

Carter, Jack, and I sat in a row on one side of the table, and Hannah and the two kids sat on the other side. I hadn't explained the purpose of my trip to the South very much, so we started there. They knew all about my dad, of course—they'd been close to Mom and she'd shared plenty of stories with them. I told them about meeting David Wilson earlier that day and about the Johnny Cash story and about David and Dad's nights together. I told them how talking to David had brought into sharper relief the abandonment our family had experienced. I didn't give many details; I just spoke in summary fashion. We all already had the outline of Bill Dodd. I was just coloring in the lines a bit. I told them I was headed to see Dad's sister next and hoping she would talk to me.

At some point in my story, Carter interrupted me—the kind of interruption that isn't rude but is sort of urgent, like he was taking a chance. Like he saw a window of opportunity that was about to close, so he hopped into it.

"Patton, I've got to say something," he blurted.

"Okay, great. That's fine," I said.

Carter looked off to the side, then back to me and continued. "I've thought this many times, but I've never been sure if I should say it to you. But I have to, because I know it's true: If your dad had not been an alcoholic, I would not be sober."

The room froze for me. The restaurant din hushed down to Carter's voice.

Carter reminded me that he'd been deep in addiction when Mom reentered Jack's life. "And here comes this expert in addiction," he said. "She knew all about Al-Anon. She knew all about Alcoholics Anonymous. She knew about different rehab options and what works and what doesn't. And she was really an expert in prayer about addiction."

Carter gestured to his dad. "He was loving me to death," he said. Jack had been too kind, giving second and third and fourth chances. "Your mom cut all that out. She was an expert in addiction, and she used that expertise to save me. I've hesitated to say this to you, because I know it didn't work in your family. I know it didn't work with your dad. And I'm sorry about that. But it worked in mine. Your mom took the insights she'd learned in all those years of trying to get your dad well, and she gave it all to me."

As Carter spoke, I looked across the table at Hannah. I looked at both of their kids.

And I understood.

The years that the locusts ate are still being returned.

Part 4

THE ONE YOU BECOME

I'm writing this in part to tell you that if you ever wonder what you've done in your life, and everyone does wonder sooner or later, you have been God's grace to me, a miracle, something more than a miracle.

— Marilynne Robinson, *Gilead*

16

The Story Machine

A COUPLE OF years ago, I sat down at our kitchen table to write a story about an epic day I'd just had with my teenage son, Henry. We'd taken a one-day road trip from San Antonio to Houston and back, stopping at Buc-ee's, catching a Spider-Man movie matinee, and then heading to the main event: watching the Denver Nuggets beat the Houston Rockets at the Toyota Center. All that made for a fantastic father-son day.

Then it leveled up. On the drive home, we stumbled into one of the best father-son conversations we'd ever had. God, sex, money, justice, relationships, family—we talked about all the big stuff. For hours. I'm not sure how Henry would rate things, but for me it was that talk that upgraded our day from fantastic to epic. Talking with, not *to*, my kids about abstract stuff is among the greatest gifts of fatherhood, not least because it's hard to manufacture the right conditions for such a conversation. It's less like setting a table and more like spotting a rare bird—I keep my spot, hope it stays a while, cherish the moment. I look forward to the next chance encounter.

The day made for a great anecdote for this book, and I could hardly wait to draft it. I got started the next morning, my heart full of father feelings. About thirty minutes in, halfway done telling the story, I was getting to the really good stuff. I paused and glanced at how much I'd written.

Almost ten pages.

Hm.

That could be a problem.

I wanted this to be a short book overall. I'd planned for part 4—the story of being a father—to be thirty to forty pages long. Here I was describing a single day of that story, and I was already using up my page count.

What about all the other days? What about all the other stories?

Do I tell you about having our first baby girl, Isabel, during graduate school in Boston? About learning to put on diapers and singing Bob Dylan lullabies to her in the middle of the night? How my wife and I got kicked out of our cozy apartment one month after Bel was born? How we freaked out and bought an overpriced, 475-square foot, third-floor South Boston condo on a no-money-down, subprime loan? How we built up over $45,000 worth of credit card debt over our first two years of parenting?

Do I tell you about how no one else we knew in Boston had kids yet and how socially isolating being a young family can be? How much it redirected our plans—how Michaela dropped out of grad school and I side-hustled so much that it took me a full decade to graduate?

Do I tell you about the time baby Bel got the rotavirus and things got scary in the middle of the night, two nights in a row? How terrified we were, holding her in our arms in the back of a taxi speeding through downtown Boston at one in the morning, then sitting with her in a crowded ER waiting room, across from a man whose hands and ankles were cuffed to his chair and who had armed guards on either side of him?

Do I tell you about watching Michaela transform into a mother? How watching her parent—observe, attend, respond—helped me learn to become a father? Or about how Michaela led us into having another baby before I thought we were ready? Then another baby right as we were preparing to move to New York City? And how utterly we disagreed about whether we could even handle having a third child? (Michaela won the argument with a line that helped me look ahead. "It's not about what makes sense right now," she said. "It's about what makes sense when I'm sixty.")

What about the time I hiked with—pushed/carried/coaxed with Skittles and Starbursts—eight-year-old Bel and five-year-old Henry up a fourteen-thousand-foot mountain? Or about when, a few years later, Henry goaded his six-year-old sister Lou into riding her broken bicycle downhill and she crashed and broke her arm? And when, a year later almost to the day, she broke her *other* arm when she tripped over a stray cat while carrying an armful of stuffed cats? And how her mom and I waaaaay underreacted to her pain, nearly to the point of neglecting to take her to the hospital, because the whole thing was so ridiculous? *Can someone really be in that much pain from tripping over a cat while carrying stuffed cats?*

What about parenting while working for one startup media company after another, changing jobs every eighteen months for most of my thirties? What about parenting our kids through two cross-country moves two summers in a row? What about living as a family of five in a tiny two-hundred-year-old house built for people the size of Hobbits? What about the year we went to a dozen or so different churches—high-church liturgical, megachurch evangelical, and everything in between—sometimes a different one on multiple consecutive Sundays, and what that taught my kids about religion (and about their dad)?

What about parenting through the loss of my mother and the indelible image of Henry, then eleven, crying in the front row of the funeral chapel?

What about teaching our firstborn how to drive? Teaching my son to play basketball? Teaching my baby girl to ride her bike, knowing I was taking off training wheels for the last time?

And those are just the canonical memories. That's not even the textured, layered everyday stuff. Bath times. Teaching them to share, do chores, apologize to each other, eat foods they don't want to eat. Arguing over what movie to watch. Debating whose farts are the smelliest. Coming home from a hard day at work to find a teenager whose day has been even harder. Coming home from a hard day at work and needing nothing so much as an hour or two of silence but finding a family full of people who want to tell you about their days. Or, on other days, coming home excited to hear about everyone's day and encountering humans who just want to sit in their own corner with their own thoughts/screens.

There are stories I could tell that make me look really bad: permitting social media too early; showing wildly inappropriate movies to my kids; being flippant, presumptuous, hypocritical, judgy; being called out by my kids for staring at my own screen, preoccupied with the news, after-hours work, finances, or this very book.

There are stories that would make me look pretty good: lotta solo cooking for my family; lotta planning trips; lotta deferring buying my own clothes and shoes so that my kids can have clothes and shoes.

So many ways to love and be loved. So many ways to hurt and be hurt. Everyday a new gauntlet of human emotions to run.

Every single day of parenting produces a story. Some days contain whole novels.

It's like I'm back in Dr. Phil's office, staring at the carpet. Only this time every story scrolling through my head is one I'm aching to tell.

Being a parent turns your life into a story machine. You capture some of them on video, in social media posts (which: *careful*), in stories shared with friends and family. You live the stories and collect them in your hearts, and that's not a typo—I mean *hearts*. You grow an extra heart for each kid, because one heart is not enough to contain all the stories you'll need to store.

If that sounds cheesy, sentimental, embarrassing, well, welcome to fatherhood.

As of this writing, I've been a father for 7,752 days. If I wrote a very short story—say, five hundred words—about some parenting thing that happened on each one of those days—and I could, I really could—I'd have a 3.8-million-word book. And that's if I focus on only my oldest child. Add in my seventeen-year-old son and his 3.1 million words of stories, and my fourteen-year-old daughter and her 2.5 million words, and we're talking about a book that is the longest book ever written.

How do you find the story of all those stories? How does a father tell the story of his own family?

• • •

Every part of this book has come out in fits and starts, or as a dad might put it, farts and sharts. My process has been to sketch out the memories as they come to mind at random, then take those memories and tie them together. "Let me be the one to stitch the white thread," sings Sturgill Simpson in

"Mint Tea," a song about domestic life, and that's been the work of this book—combining the fabric scraps of my life into something coherent and whole.

But my own family's story requires a different approach. I cannot be the fabricator of this one. Our story does not belong to me alone.

Parenting is unlike most other stories you experience in your life, because as your kids age, you come to a gradual realization: You are not the main character. As the story progresses, sometimes you're barely a character at all—you move from upstage to downstage to the front row, though at other times they'd rather you sit in the back. Or wait in the lobby.

Parenting is an epic tale where you begin as the hero, then keep taking lesser and lesser roles. Every now and then, you're called back on stage, and you gotta be ready to take your cue. But you also gotta not be a prima donna during those long stretches where the right move is to watch and wait.

Parenting decenters you. This is a tough realization to accept, because you are obviously the center of your own world. We talk about this like it's a bad thing—*people are so self-centered*—when it's just the basic fact of existence. The universe is a 360-degree arc carved out from each of us. We see the world from within our own bodies and minds. Being ourselves is what grounds us in this world; being ourselves gives us a starting point for everything we take in.

Yet over time, a self does need to be decentered. Each of us must come to understand that we're actually part of a network that both needs us *and* can exist without us. A decentered self finds the balance of those twin realities.

In my experience, nothing provides an education in decentering quite like parenting.

Recently, I gave one of my kids some bad advice. I didn't realize it at the time—I thought for sure I was telling them exactly what they needed to hear. They were going through something painful, and I felt I had the situation sized up perfectly. I saw with 100 percent clarity what the kid needed to do, and I told them. But as I proffered my fatherly wisdom, I could see their eyes glazing over. They thought I was wrong, missing the point. Which only made me stress my words all the more. *I am Parent! You are Child! Learn from me!*

That went about as well as you would imagine.

Later, I overheard them telling a friend about the painful thing they'd been going through, and the situation sounded different from what I'd understood before. It was like hearing news from another country. The penny dropped: The advice I'd been giving wasn't just wrong; it was irrelevant. I'd absorbed their experience into my own, and my advice was really all about me—I had been talking to myself. When my kid first talked to me about it, the better fathering move would have been for me to just listen, full stop, and not say anything at all. I was not a character in their story at that point, much less a director.

Parenting is a lifelong opportunity to learn that it is not about you. Yet that does not mean you can withdraw. You have to show up in the stories that are happening all around you, and you have to learn the right way to be present in those stories—just enough you, at just the right times. Our influence over our child's story is profound, but it is also a gradual, inexorable, necessary diminishment.

That is the gift and the challenge of parenting.

• • •

My friend Tara observed to me the other day that most of the book I've been writing has been in fulfillment of one of the Ten Commandments: Honor your father and your mother. That verse can be/has been put to all sorts of bad use in the wrong hands, but it's not about simple obedience or reverence. It's about giving someone their due. The word in Exodus translated as "honor" has to do with "weight," like the weight on an ancient scale. Giving parents honor means weighing them rightly, according to who and what they are.

It doesn't say "honor your children." In the end, it is not my job to weigh Bel, Henry, and Lou.

They are the ones who will be weighing me.

17

Why Dads Are So Cheesy

WHEN YOUR FIRST baby is born, you are born right along with them. You may think you know who you are on that day, but you do not. Your essential identity is about to change from the inside out. You are going to become a parent.

Biologically speaking, sure, you are already a parent, but only in the same way that your newborn is already a human. You've both got some developing to do. This development will take time and effort—crawl, stand, walk, talk, gain reason. Eventually, with enough patience and persistence, grit, and grace, you will become a full-fledged parent.

You will not be the person you were before.

The last day I was not a father was May 21, 2003. Michaela and I were living in Boston. The day before, I had called up a new friend named Joe, who worked for the Boston Red Sox. I'd asked him for tickets to that night's game. The Yankees were in town, and Red Sox ace Pedro Martinez was scheduled to pitch, but that's not why I wanted to go to the game. Michaela was great with child, and her due date had come and gone more than a week before. We had tried all the things you can try to induce labor—spicy foods, long walks, sex. The baby stayed tucked in Michaela's tummy, which got bigger, heavier, firmer. We could feel the tick of every second. Our future family was taking forever to get started.

We'd heard tell of a local myth: Fenway Park sends expectant women into labor. I was a graduate student and we were living on a shoestring budget. Tickets were not in that budget, but Joe had assured me we could call him for a Fenway favor anytime.

I remember Joe saying yes, and I remember us taking the T to Kenmore Square. I remember having fish and chips and a Harpoon IPA before the game. (Michaela had just one sip.) I remember exactly where we sat: twelve rows behind the first-base dugout. I remember our Fenway seat mates joking about how the baby inside Michaela looked like it was ready to come out and pitch cleanup. I remember that Pedro Martinez was a late scratch, and so the Red Sox tossed a mix of arms at the Yankees, fell behind early, had a five-run eighth inning, and won 10–7.

I remember all that, but I do not remember what it was like to be the people Michaela and I were on that day.

The record shows that Michaela was a proofreader. I was a PhD student in religion and literature at BU. We loved Boston and missed Colorado. We were up to our waists in debt, and we'd soon be up to the crowns of our heads. I know those basic facts, but I cannot recall much about how it felt to be pre-father Patton. I don't know how I arranged my days and set my priorities. I don't remember how it felt to want what I wanted from my life at that point. The baby changed everything from the inside out.

The Fenway-as-pitocin trick worked. A few hours after the game, Michaela started feeling birth pangs, and we drove to Mount Auburn Hospital to cross one of life's great thresholds.

I spent most of Michaela's daylong labor not knowing how to be present in the moment. Michaela's mom was with us in the delivery room, and she ended up between Michaela and me, closer to her daughter's face. I stayed near the belly, looking up at my wife struggling through birth pangs.

This is the first lesson of fatherhood. Sometimes, you will have nothing to offer.

But when the work is done and the baby is safely born, they will let you cut the cord, which is kind of them.

When they put our baby girl into my arms, I could have been holding anyone's baby. She did not yet have a name—it would be a day or two before we settled on Isabel Nicole. She was larger than I thought she'd be, as if the extra womb time had turned her into a toddler. I worried that we'd missed a special phase, like when you get a puppy at eight months instead of eight weeks. But Bel, as she soon became known, was breathing and wailing, and the nurses said she was beautiful. I chose to believe everything was as it should be.

Still, how do you hold a baby? I don't mean the technique. I mean the spirit of the thing. I'd heard all these stories of babies being slipped into a new father's arms and how he looks at his newborn in wonder and awe. I'd talked to other young dads who were gobsmacked by the experience of holding their child for the first time. I'd heard tales of tears streaming down dads' faces. I'd expected a surge of joy, reverence, *love*. Is that what I was feeling? How would I know? What does fatherly love feel like?

I spent the next few days and weeks trying to be what a new father is supposed to be. I pitched in. I took overnight shifts. I fed bottles. I changed diapers. All these actions felt pretty damn tricky the first time I did them and like second nature by the third or fourth time. I walked Bel back and forth in my arms, lullabying her with "Shelter from the Storm." I sat and laid her on my knees and peered at her as she grimaced back at me. I smelled her lovely head and ran my thumbs along the soles of her adorable feet.

But what I didn't do was the main thing I'd been expecting to do all those months when Michaela was pregnant. I didn't have big feelings. I wasn't overwhelmed with a father's love. I *loved* our baby, for sure. No doubt about it. Conceptually, yes, most def, I was doing the fatherly love thing. I was committed to this child.

Yet I'd expected . . . something more. A heart swell of some kind. A certain overwhelming. But I wasn't feeling much of anything yet. I could be dutiful, but I couldn't . . . well, what? Was I not connecting with my child? Was I not loving her the way a father was supposed to love? I wasn't sure.

One day a couple of weeks after Bel was born, I rode my bike along the Charles River, thinking about all this and wondering what was wrong with my heart. Maybe I didn't know how to be a father. My dad had been like an unfilled-in outline of a father my whole life. Maybe he'd shaped me into someone who couldn't feel father feelings.

I was determined to do a good job. But I figured I'd have a surge of good, strong, palpable emotion to sustain my efforts. I remember pedaling that path and trying to accept that maybe my heart was broken. Not in the sense of being sad, but in the sense of actually not functioning.

Was I going to love my child? Sure. But was I going to *feel* love? When?

• • •

Eighteen years later, I sat at home by myself on my living room couch in San Antonio, Texas, and I bawled my eyes out. No one else was home, so I was free to cry the ugliest cry I'd ever cried. I was free to wail at the ceiling, tears streaming down my face as I lamented my separation from Bel.

Three hours earlier, I'd dropped off her and her mom at the airport in Austin, and they were flying to New Mexico, where Bel was moving for college. I'd been crying off and on for much of those three hours—on the way out of the airport, I had nearly crashed my car because I was crying so hard I couldn't see through the windshield. I called my dear friend Rob, who lives in Austin, and asked him to come to an emergency lunch with me. He obliged. Rob and I ate and talked about being dads—a father of four girls, the man knows his stuff. I felt comforted. Then I got in my car and headed back to San Antonio and started crying again.

At some point during my cry, I swiped my phone open and saw that my wife had sent me a photo of Bel and me hugging goodbye. Then I did something I almost never do, which is share that photo on Instagram, along with a bunch of words. My post read, in part, as follows:

> *Here's what you do: You have a baby, probably before you are ready. B/c there is no "ready." Even while still at the hospital, people ask you, "Did you love her at first sight?" and you wonder if something is wrong with you. There is wonder, and there is worry. There is exhaustion, and there is all sorts of hope. But love? Fatherly love? Maybe—but what does that feel like? How do you know when you have it? Her mom is already doing everything right, right off the bat. But what about you? Can you love this person as well and true as you ought?*
>
> *18 years and two months later—that's 218 months, which is far too few months—you've amassed all the evidence you'll ever need. It's not in the photos, and it's not even in the memories. It's somewhere you can't quite place but that is also everyplace. You love her, no doubt. She knows it, too.*

And her knowing it is the best part—her trusting your love is the reward for loving her.

I don't remember when the feelings of fatherly love clicked in. It didn't take long once I stopped worrying about it. But not all of us have hearts made ready for parenting. Just because you have a kid, that doesn't mean you get that parenting heart. Sometimes it has to grow. Sometimes you have to help it grow. Nature helps us a lot but does not get us all the way there. Love needs seeding, watering, pruning. It needs time.

With each child, a new heart grows. I love each of my three children very much, and I love them differently, as if I am loving each of them with a sui generis heart made especially for them. That's three different hearts crammed within the space of my one actual heart. Which is why dads are so very cheesy—kids make us that way by creating tons of pressure on our chests. Our hearts are compressed mush.

Case in point: Last night, we watched *Pitch Perfect* as a family, and I cried at the end.

Pitch Perfect is not a tearjerker. It's a musical comedy in the form of a sports movie, where an underdog college acapella team wins the national championship. The movie builds to a big, feel-good ending with a show-stopping musical number that resolves a handful of storylines at once: The heroine, Beca, has a breakthrough performance; her team beats the bad guys; the romantic leads finally get together, and in the flush of victory we see them have their first kiss. The backbone to all this is the remixed, nostalgic sound of Simple Minds' "Don't You (Forget About Me)," made famous by the closing scene of *The Breakfast Club*.

But none of that is what makes me cry. None of that is meant to make anyone cry. What makes me cry is a single shot of Beca's father, a shot that lasts 1.6 seconds.

We learn early on about the conflict between this father-daughter pair—him a comparative literature professor, her an aspiring music producer. Beca is self-taught and ripping with talent, but her dad, all weak beard and receding hairline, is an asshole. He doesn't see his daughter's gifts. He sees only a ridiculous kid who is not taking college seriously.

This storyline is thin. The movie doesn't give us any other context for this family. Beca's mom is never mentioned. Beca and her dad have just three scenes together, and in each one, all they do is bicker. The movie keeps it basic. Beca is cool. Beca's dad is an asshole.

My head knows this storyline sucks, but my heart doesn't care what my head thinks, because I am a full-on dad. Dads don't get to tell their hearts what to think. Dad hearts have a mind of their own.

In the final scene, when Beca is having her big moment on stage, when she's breaking through and winning everyone over, we see a quick shot of Beca's dad in the crowd. He's there! He loves his girl! He sees who she really is! Beaming with 1.6 seconds of pride, he calls out, "Way to go, Beca!"

It's pretty dumb. But every time I see it, I burst into tears. Even writing this description of it, I'm tearing up all over again.

• • •

Our youngest child, Louisa, woke up a few minutes ago and came downstairs. I'm sitting down here on the couch right now working on this book, and she glances over my shoulder to see what I'm writing.

"You're writing about watching *Pitch Perfect* last night?" she groans. I ignore her and keep typing. I am mid-thought and mid-sentence. Lou stays perched and keeps reading.

"Oh wait, you're writing about *crying*?!?! Ugh. Dad! You cried at the end of *Pitch Perfect*? You're lucky I had gone to bed already before the movie ended. I would have laughed at you."

Yes, true. Lou slipped off to bed before the end, and so I got to cry without Lou making fun of me. That's become a thing between us. Some small thing moves me to tears, and Lou is there like Nelson in *The Simpsons*: "Ha-ha!" (One thing you can't expect the first time you hold your newborn baby is that one of the great joys of life will be having them make fun of you.)

But Lou has herself to blame for my teariness. She's part of the problem, along with Bel and Henry. My kids have made me full of feeling.

In my pre-dad years, I would often get accused of being a cynic. It irked me, but I sorta understood why people thought of me that way. I questioned everything. I was a bit emo, without the cool clothes and hair to show for it. All my favorite movies and books were either dark and disturbing or dry and distant. I talked a lot about how I hated sentimentality. I went around quoting Oscar Wilde: "A sentimentalist is one who desires to have the luxury of emotion without paying for it" (from the essay "The Critic as Artist"). I was skeptical of stories that went straight for my chest. *Give me something to think about*, I'd say, *not something to feel*.

But then you become a parent, and you start spending vast amounts of time with humans for whom you bear all responsibility. You bandage a lot of knees. You make a lot of meals for other people, and you find it delightful to make things they like. As they get older and become more aware of what this world is, you start carrying a lot more hope and talking about hope and modeling hope, because you want the people you have the most influence over to be people of hope. You want them not to feel the way you feel on your worst days. You want them to think well of other people and of the world we're sharing with them.

You want their hearts to be open. So you open your own heart.

18

Dad Lessons

AS OF THIS writing, Michaela and I are the parents of a twenty-one-year-old, a seventeen-year-old, and a fourteen-year-old. We've been at this for a while. Last night, I asked her, "What do you know about parenting now that you wish you had known when, say, our third kid was born? When you were the mother of a newborn, a three-year-old, and a six-year-old?"

"Everything," she said, without a moment of hesitation. "I wish I knew back then everything I know now."

But that, of course, is not the way this works. You don't start parenting with an understanding of what parenting is. You work from instincts, a newborn baby goat stumbling around in matted fur. Becoming a solid parent takes as much training as becoming a surgeon, except surgeons-in-training work on cadavers and get years of instruction. Parents-in-training are given real live human subjects on the first day. Parenting is its own pedagogy. Each home is its own unique classroom—indeed, each individual kid is their own classroom, because what works for one doesn't work for another. Most terrifying of all, you can never really know whether the parenting moves you're making are the right ones until you've already made them.

You leave the maternity ward knowing your child needs food and clothing and safety, and you can figure those things out pretty well so long as nothing strange comes up. (Note: Something strange will come up). As the days and weeks turn into months and years, they need different kinds of food, clothing, and safety and then also education and medicine and discipline and play and friends and then better friends and then instruction in all kinds of things— tying shoes and riding bikes and cleaning dishes and making beds and washing hair and washing genitals and covering odors and dressing for the weather and crossing the street and answering the front door (or not answering the front door) and pulling weeds and loading the dishwasher the right way and speaking to adults and speaking on phones like a normal human being and doing homework and spending money and saving money and making money and finding coping strategies with all manner of things that happen on all manner of days.

On the daily for almost two decades, you keep realizing, "Oh, right. I need to teach them how to do this too." Only sometimes you're teaching them to navigate things you haven't yet figured out how to navigate for yourself. Then, as they get older and the generational gap between you and them widens, you also realize they're having experiences that not only do you not know how to explain but that you've also never actually had, using language you've never even heard. And this is all before they even get seriously online.

All of parenting, across all the years that your kids are in your care, is a lot like putting on diapers for the first time. How is it possible that you don't know how to do this thing that you now have to do? (How is it possible that you don't know the oil doesn't go in the gas tank?) And you have to do it *now*, because there is poop and there is urine and their skin might already be chafing and now they feel the cool breeze of the fan overheard and they are peeing again and it's straight into the air and you're not sure whether to dodge the pee or try to contain the pee but there is no time to decide, there is only time to act.

From diapers to the digital diaspora, you follow your instincts. Sometimes you trust those instincts, sometimes you don't, but instinct is what you have to work with either way. You hope it all comes out okay. You guess your way forward. You feel like you are not up to the task. You pray for wisdom. You second-guess yourself. You talk to other parents about how they're doing what they're doing, and sometimes they answer with a kind of confidence and conviction that makes you second-guess yourself even more. You will find, later, that those parents did not really know what they were doing, either. They were figuring it out on the go, because that is how parenting works.

One of our kids is now an adult who attends college seven hundred miles away. One new lesson we've learned of late is that navigating health care systems from seven hundred miles away is very complicated. You might as well be navigating health care systems in another country. Every parent who has had a kid go to college out of state comes to understand this. It's another basic fact of parenting, as common as getting kids to eat new foods. But you don't find out that you need to know how to do this until you need to know how to do it. And when you need to know how to do it, you'll be pulling your hair out, because doing it is hard. It's like looking for a pink paper clip in the middle of the night in a dark room full of multicolored paper clips. Then, when you talk to other parents who are also navigating long-distance health care systems, their response is some form of *I KNOW, RIGHT?!?!* They've all gone through something like the same experience, yet you've never heard about it before.

The mercy in all of this is that so long as you keep showing up, so long as you keep trying, you're probably doing a good-enough job. Nature takes care of so many things. And of course, you are not the only good influence on your children's lives—they will find wisdom from many sources, not least of all their own experience.

But if you're anything like me, you don't live every day comfortable in the knowledge that it's going to turn out okay. You live in the uncertainty of not knowing whether you're doing what you need to be doing. You live with the awareness that you are the parent they get.

• • •

Fatherhood is a leap of faith. It requires believing that you can be a force for good in your children's lives. That's not always easy, because you are you.

Consider:

One Easter Sunday morning when Bel was six years old, not long after she'd finished looking for Easter eggs, I told her that the Easter Bunny wasn't real. Or the Tooth Fairy. Or Santa Claus. Those are fine things to tell your kid, but it happened all at once, with no warning. Over the course of about thirty seconds, all of Bel's favorite mystical gift-giving creatures were rendered into plain ol' Mom and Dad. It felt right to me in the moment, but by the end of the day I wanted to rewind the clock.

Now, I told her this only because she backed me into a corner. "Dad, remember how you told me you would never lie to me?" she said, then proceeded to ask me for the truth about who had put her Easter basket together that morning. But still, she was six and I was thirty-five, and I probably should have discerned that the blunt force of too much reality would leave a mark. Alas, I did not.

Bel seemed okay with it at first. But later that afternoon, on our way home from an Easter dinner with extended family, she was crying in the back seat as she told us of the pain of being around her Easter Bunny–believing cousins.

"It's hard to be the only one who knows what everyone else believes isn't true," she said, at six years old.

It would not be the last time I ushered one of my kids into existential anxiety.

Then there's this: I have never had any sense of what is appropriate to show children. I scared the bejesus out of Bel by showing her a truly disturbing movie called *The Babadook* one time, a good twenty-five years before she was ready to be that disturbed. I showed the raunchy teenage comedy *Superbad* to Henry when he was too young—or at least, I showed him about thirty minutes of it, at which point he asked me to turn it off because it felt inappropriate *to him*. I also tried to show him the hilarious Netflix show *Big Mouth*, which is about kids going through puberty from the perspective of the kids. I figured we'd laugh together at jokes about morning wood and wet dreams, clearing the air for us to talk comfortably about anything pertaining to sexuality. Instead, just a few jokes into the first episode, Henry turned to me and said, "Dad, there is no way I can watch this with you."

Also, were it not for Michaela, I would walk around the house naked a lot, including in front of my teenage girls. My wife put a stop to that several years back, for which I'm grateful. Until I was told otherwise, it did not occur to me that it might be problematic for them to see their father in all his glory.

Then there's practical know-how and my utter lack of it. I mentioned earlier that I've picked up some basic competencies, and that is true, but my chops remain meager. I am still no good with engines. Lawn care is my enemy. Finding a wall stud is guesswork, despite practicing every method known to man. My kids have hilarious (to them) stories of me trying to teach them how to fish. Buying used cars? It's like pulling a slot machine—I put in all the money I have on my person, close my eyes, and hope for the best.

Actually, that last part isn't true. I've become decent at buying used cars, because pain is a good teacher. Once, after Michaela and I had poured thousands of dollars—Visa's dollars, to be precise, borrowed at 21 percent interest—into a rickety Jeep Cherokee we shouldn't have bought in the first place, she did the math and found that we could have leased a fancy new car for the same amount of money we'd spent trying to keep the old Jeep running for three years. Did I wise up about used car purchases at that point? Nope. It took another fifteen years or so—another half dozen lemons—to settle on a sensible approach.

Which gets us to money. I've gotten much better at managing it after years of unlearning and retraining. But it's been an arduous journey. Every time I review our finances, which I do almost every Sunday afternoon whether I want to or not, I am fighting demons of insecurity.

And the demons aren't just my own. I'm still fighting Dad's demons too.

• • •

In the spring of my senior year of high school, my father gave me some very expensive advice.

I'd surprised my parents by getting into the University of Alabama. My grades and test scores were fine, so the admission itself wasn't surprising, but I hadn't told them I was applying. We had not talked about college at all—I remember zero conversations—and the only reason I'd applied to Alabama was because I loved their football team and my high school guidance counselor told me I needed to apply somewhere.

When I shared the acceptance letter with Dad, he grimaced, then laughed. "Well, son, congratulations, that's really cool," he said, "but of course there is no way you are going." He laughed some more and squinted at me, like we were in on a joke together. What a funny thing I'd done!

"What do you mean?" I asked. "I want to go."

He asked if I knew how much it cost. I did not. He asked whether I had a plan for paying for college. I did not. It had not occurred to me until that moment that paying for college was something I needed a plan for. Colleges had scholarships and something called grants, a synonym for *free*. Plus, Kaysie had gone to college somehow, way off in Missouri. I figured these things took care of themselves.

"College is very expensive, son," he told me. "I hope you weren't expecting me to pay for it." I assured him I was not, and that was true. I simply had not given it a single thought.

Sons follow in their father's footsteps whether they mean to or not. For Dad, money was not something you thought about very much, and it certainly was not something you talked about. You might pray for money. You might ask people to let you borrow money. But mostly you avoided the subject. My dad and I had talked about paying for college even less than we'd talked about going to college. If we'd talked about going to college zero times, we'd talked about paying for college a negative number of times. We were in debt to the conversation about paying for college.

A day or two later, I came home from school to find a Free Application for Financial Student Aid on the kitchen table. Next to it was a Visa application. Dad was home early that day, and he came downstairs and saw me looking at the forms. "Good, yes, let's talk about those," he said and picked up and waved around the student aid application, which he called a FAFSA. He said it like it was an actual word, one I should have known already. He pointed out how short the FAFSA was, how easy to fill out. "The FAFSA," he said, "is how the government helps you pay for college."

"Okay, so the government *does* help you pay for college," I said. "I thought so."

"Sure, son. Didn't you notice how much out-of-state tuition costs at the University of Alabama? It's insane. Nobody actually pays it, though. Colleges make it impossible on purpose. It's a whole system. But the government will loan you the money for it and make it really easy for you to pay it back."

Dad's voice warmed as he talked, like he was only just now realizing the genius of our nation's system. "You don't even have to worry about paying them back while you're in school," he said. "Some of the money is subsidized, and some of it's not, but most of it will be. Either way, they won't make you pay any of it back while you're enrolled in college, so you don't have to worry. And then after college, you can be in forbearance for a long time."

I didn't understand many of the key terms he was using. He kept talking.

"And they'll give you more than you need to cover tuition. Every semester, you'll get a refund check sent to you to cover all your living expenses." I didn't understand that, either, but it sounded like cash would be coming to me, which was terrific news.

"So that's the FAFSA. You'll fill this out today and then it'll take a while to find out how much you'll get. I'm sure it'll be plenty, more than enough. And you don't have to worry about it as long as you are in school." I was a bit lost, but the main message was coming through: "don't have to worry." College was paid for. Awesome.

But, Dad said, while that refund cash was going to help, it might take a while for it to come, and it wouldn't be enough to pay for all that I was going to need. He picked up the Visa application and waved it before me.

"You're eighteen years old," said my father. "You're an adult. It's time for you to have your own credit card."

"I need a credit card for college?"

"College costs more than just tuition." He grinned his grin of frustration. He was shorter than I was but somehow smiling over me. "There are class fees, and parking fees, and lots of expensive books to buy. You won't believe what they'll charge for these books, son. Did you think you could pay for all that by working at Chick-fi-A? Did you think *I* was going to pay for it?"

I assured him I had not. Dad smiled harder, and he shook his head, exasperated.

"You're going to need a credit card," he said firmly, resolving the matter. "And look, they sent this directly to *you*."

He held up the Visa envelope, and yes, I could see my name on the front: Mr. Patton Dodd. Visa had bestowed upon me the honor of this invitation to apply, complete with "OFFER INSIDE!" stamped in big blue type. Dad explained that Visa was offering a full year with no interest for first-time applicants. I did not know what "interest" meant, but I intuited it all to be a continuation of the "don't have to worry" theme.

Dad reached up and rubbed my shoulder, as if to help massage in the information.

"This is a really good deal," he said. "You can get all you need to start college—books, school supplies—and it doesn't really cost you anything."

"It doesn't cost me anything? So they'll pay for the books?"

"No, son. I mean borrowing the money from Visa won't cost you anything. You can't usually borrow money for free, with no interest, but with this offer, you can. It's a good deal."

I was having a hard time feeling as excited by the offer as Dad was.

"Okay, Dad. I'll think about applying."

"Oh, okay." He let the application letter fall to the kitchen table. "You think about it, then." There was hurt in his voice. "While you think about it, also think about how else you're going to pay for your books and the other things you need."

He let my thinking hang in the air for a moment.

Then he said, "You need a plan, son. I'm trying to help you build a plan."

That night, I filled out both applications and put them in their self-addressed stamped envelopes. My dad celebrated by heading out to the store and bringing home shrimp and cocktail sauce.

• • •

When my dad was giving strong financial advice, he was, I can see now, bluffing. I called his bluff—I took his advice and followed it for years and years. Throughout college, when I struggled to make ends meet, Dad would encourage me to take out more loans. He had me take out additional midsemester loans. A couple of times, he borrowed my borrowed money. Perhaps if you hadn't read the earlier part of this book, you may have thought that I would have put a stop to that. You may have thought that I would have known better. But now you know that I did not. Even after I did know better, I didn't put a stop to it. I kept following his advice for a long, long time.

My father's bluster and confidence were persuasive. Dad bluster leaves an impression, because dads are supposed to know how to do things. They're supposed to be competent, to show you how the world works. They make footsteps; you follow them.

But one of the most important things dads need to know how to do is to *not know*. They need to be able to say "I don't know." They need to come to terms with their own incompetencies and find non-bluffing ways to fill those gaps in knowledge. When they aren't sure how to solve a problem for their kids, they oughta say so. Maybe dad and kid can find a way through the problem together.

Fatherhood is an education in all sorts of things. You're always being confronted with something new that no one prepared you for. You have to learn to learn. You can read books and search websites and ask others for advice. But first you must admit that you are experiencing the not-knowing. That fear you feel when your daughter or son asks a question you don't know how to answer? Happens all the time. Uncertainty is part of what fathering is. Wise fathers get used to it, and they don't bluff.

• • •

Of course—and fortunately for me—the most important things you need to learn as a father are not practical. The most important things you need to learn are about you.

One Saturday evening a few years back, Michaela and I sat down on our back porch with two drinks in hand and four or five blessedly empty hours stretching out before us. I needed those hours like the drought needs rain. It'd been a long day at the end of a long week at the end of a long month. We'd not had a proper date night since Lord knows when. Henry and Bel were both out of town. We'd just gotten home from dropping off Lou to hang out with some new friends at a minor league baseball game way, way, way across town—but the drive was worth it, because now we had a night to ourselves.

Within a minute of sitting down on the porch, both our phones dinged. I groaned and looked at my screen. It was a text from Lou: "This isn't fun."

"Well, that's too bad," I said aloud and started to text something along those lines into the group thread.

"Hold on," said Michaela. "Something is going on here."

"What's going on is that she needs to stick it out," I said, all firm and fatherly. Every kid goes through a night that does not live up to their expectations. Was she just bored from baseball? That's ridiculous. Did she not like her new friends as much as she thought? Too bad. Were the friends being a bit mean? Whatever. Suffering through awkward social situations is valuable. And doesn't she need to toughen up? What a great chance to learn a lesson.

I was saying things along these lines, making my case, but I could tell Michaela was tuning me out. She was thinking of all the contextual details: how Lou's night had been arranged in the first place, who she was with, and what she'd been going through at school the last few weeks. Michaela started texting with Lou on the side, leaving me out of the thread and asking her to say more about what was happening.

I talked for a few moments more about the value of suffering, then tried another angle, explaining just how desperately I needed a couple of hours with my wife on the back porch. Michaela kept texting. I argued that it would create a terrible precedent if we saved our kid from this situation. It would send the wrong signal—that we'll hop into action at the slightest complaint. Is that what we want our kids to believe? Do we want to coddle them? And again, don't we desperately need this date night?

"So let's not go get her," I finished. "This is going to be fine."

Michaela stood up. "I'm going to go pick her up," she said.

I went along, frustrated and planning to share with Lou all the insights I'd just shared with Michaela. Soon, Michaela would see that I was right. Our kid had just been whining. And Lou would feel bad about ruining our date night. Our night would be ruined, but at least everyone would learn a lesson.

When we got to where we were going, we saw Lou standing on the curb waiting for us. The look on her face was all I needed to know that I was wrong. There was more to the story.

On the drive home, we heard about what'd been happening that night, about just how badly our girl had been treated by these new friends who were anything but. I was so glad we'd airlifted her out of the situation. I was so glad Michaela had ears to hear.

I was so glad for yet another chance to learn the most fundamental, perpetual lesson of fatherhood; the lesson I hope to remain learning for the rest of my life: I have so much to learn.

19

The Future of Fatherhood

ONE LATE-SUMMER NIGHT several years ago, I was at the house of my friend Jim, whose oldest child, Zach, had just graduated from high school. The mood in the home was celebratory but wistful. This tight-knit family of five was bracing for the boy's move to a college many hundreds of miles away.

We'd always talked about movies, Zach and I, and that night we got to talking about Wes Anderson films. I asked him what he thought of *Rushmore*, Anderson's second feature, from 1998.

"Never seen it," he said.

I was flabbergasted at this display of fatherly negligence. I look over at his dad. "What's wrong with you? You've never shown your son *Rushmore*?"

Jim responded with a line—and a pained tone—that has been ringing in my head ever since. "Turns out that eighteen years is not enough time," he said.

Later, I asked Jim to say more about what he wished he still had time to share with his son: movies, concerts, backpacking trails, whatever. But he told me he really wasn't thinking of missed opportunities. He was thinking about how deeply he'd settled into this life with his son and two daughters and how he was awakening to the reality that it was all changing. As each child left home, a season of fathering would come to a close. He had no idea how to prepare for the next season.

How do you be the parent of someone who lives far away? More to the point, how do you be the parent of someone who now needs a less persistent form of parenting?

How do you father someone you've fathered?

Those first eighteen years of raising kids are action-packed, which makes them capacity-limited. It's the same period of life when we're trying to build careers, get more education and certification, come to terms with our own childhoods, maintain a house and car, strengthen our religious and spiritual impulses and communities, save money, go on adventures and vacations, engage with politics, pay taxes, have healthy bodies, make and keep adult friends, cook and clean, and maybe, just maybe, get some rest.

These high-intensity years are also the same ones that our kids are absorbing everything, needing everything. These are the years when they are most interested in us, willing and able to absorb whatever influence we can give. Then those years begin to wane. Even while they're still living at home, kids begin to be more on their own. They build appendages to their lives at home. They have thoughts and experiences that we don't get access to. They have extended experiences of other families, and those experiences put their home life into relief. A lot of *aha*s and *oh shit*s happen for them in these years. *Aha, so that's what was going on with my parents back then!* Or: *Oh shit, I can't believe that's what was going on with my parents back then!* Your children may discover that they don't like the same things you like. They may not feel about things how you feel about things. They may have completely different interests, strange (to you) tastes in music or food. They may have different—*gasp*—politics. They may have different—*WTF*—religious convictions.

Right as they're navigating the world on their own, our capacity for parenting begins to grow. We have more time on our hands, in part because our kids are around less. We're going for walks. We're volunteering. We're watching too much television. And we're wanting, more than ever, to spend lots and lots and lots of time with our kids.

We've made a million investments in our children. Now we want a return. Our need for them hits a peak around the time their need for us hits a valley. Right around the time you're most ready to live in the present as a parent, you find out that you've been preparing all along for your parenting future, and it's not much like the present at all.

My son, Henry, graduates next year, and he hopes to move to another part of the country. I'm glad I've already had the experience of watching one of my kids leave, because at least I know the hardship that is coming. When Bel left, I knew I'd miss her, of course, but there was so much more I didn't know. Whole new dimensions of our relationship that

I was not prepared for. Whole new kinds of parenting—and *not* parenting. New ways of relating to an adult child who sometimes needs you to be more peer than parent.

It's very hard to recalibrate to this stage, but recalibration is what is called for. My relationship with each of my kids needs to change. It's going to keep happening as these children of mine keep adulting—finding partners, getting married, having kids, having bosses, having whole weeks and then whole months I may not need to know all that much about. Whole parts of their life where I may have no role at all beyond the role that I've already played.

"There is no such thing as reproduction," writes Andrew Solomon in the opening to *Far from the Tree: Parents, Children, and the Search for Identity* (Scribner, 2013). When you raise children, you're not reproducing yourself—you're producing an entirely distinct entity, one that is very much not you. Early on, you're the expert on that entity, the boss of all its ways. You've wiped its butt, sopped its snot, worried over its every jot and tittle. But then the entity becomes a full person, and your familiarity begins to wane. You might take offense at the waning, but that won't get you anywhere you want to go. You best recalibrate. Get curious. Get to know the person you raised.

• • •

One day back in 1998, a few weeks before I married Michaela, my mom called and said she needed to get something off her chest. She'd been talking to her best friend, Connie, who had helped her see something hard but true.

"I was talking to her about how special my relationship with you has been these past few years," she said. "All our long walks in the neighborhood. All the nights we sat there eating stovetop popcorn and wondering if Dad was going to make it home. All the things you'd share with me, and all the things you'd let me share with you."

She told me that Connie stopped her at some point and said, "Dawn, you know this is all going to change, right? It *has* to change." Connie said she knew how much Mom had loved being the most important confidant in my life. "But you won't be that person any longer. You can't be. You need to become second to Michaela.

"You have to let him go," Connie stressed. "And in case he doesn't see this, either, you need to tell him that you're letting him go."

Mom told me this story through tears, and she apologized for the tears. "I want you to know that it's really okay," she said. "You're going to call me less often, and that's okay. You're going to depend on Michaela more than me, and that's okay. It won't change how I feel about you. I love you, and I will always cherish our relationship. But it has to change now."

At the time, I felt Connie was overstating things. But she was right, and Mom was right. Our relationship changed. Distance grew between us. And it was okay.

My mom's way of letting go actually performed a neat trick: It made our relationship more likely to endure. It made the connection between us elastic instead of brittle. I'd get real busy at times, lose touch, call her less, offer infrequent updates. On the phone all day at work, picking it up for personal calls felt like just another chore.

But when I did call my mom in the years before she passed, no matter how long it had been since I had called, she'd always answer the same way: "How is my sweet boy?" I never heard one hint of resentment from her.

I've kept my mom's model of recalibration in mind throughout my years of parenting. I assumed that I would follow her lead someday, and I looked forward to being that noble. But now my own time of letting go of my kids is getting closer. Indeed, it is already here, and I feel myself not recalibrating but clinging. I feel myself wanting to parent my older kids harder now than I did when they were younger. I want to direct, shape, hold. I want to dictate how we call and text and FaceTime, for it to happen on my preferred terms in my preferred timing.

That is not the way. It's not how I need to enter this next stage of fatherhood. Because I want the next stage, and I want the one after that, whatever the stage may hold. I want these relationships to go on and on. I may find that I am less helpful to my children as they age. I may find that I'm less relevant to whatever they're facing. But I hope I have enough wisdom and heft that they always turn to me for something. I hope I always have something to offer. If nothing else, I hope they turn to me for presence.

I hope fathering never ends.

• • •

One summer weekend a couple of years back, I had a taste of family heaven. It was one I did not expect, and it was one I could not have planned. It came in a season of high anxiety for me—repeated challenges and failures in my work, related sleeplessness for weeks on end, unexpected big expenses on the home front, the grind of a midlife career change for Michaela, and more. We were worn down to absolute nubs.

On the Friday of that weekend, Michaela, Henry, and Lou came with me to a work event in a neighborhood near downtown San Antonio. A cross section of our city was there, an exhilarating mishmash of community. We stayed late—we were some of the last to go because Henry had also brought a bunch of friends, and they started playing pickup basketball with some neighborhood kids. I joined them and we hooped until late, then drove everyone home, stopping at Whataburger along our way. When we dropped off the last kid, Henry's friend Javi, we heard him let out a "Whoop!" as he walked to the front door—as in "What a great night!"—and we agreed. Henry and I finally got home around midnight and remembered that game 4 of the NBA Finals had happened, so we stayed up extra late and watched it on delay.

Already this would have made for a rich weekend memory, but things were just getting started. Early the next morning, we rose early to head back downtown for a political march. We carried our signs, chanted with the crowd. We made a beeline for our congressman when we spotted him in the mix, shaking his hand and getting a photo. We ate empanadas afterward at one of my favorite San Antonio spots.

We got home just in time for Henry to don a rented tuxedo. He was on court for a quinceañera that night, the most San Antonio thing possible for a fifteen-year-old to do. We took amazing photos of him mugging for the camera and dribbling a basketball in a tux.

While Henry's outfit was coming together, Lou had recruited her mom to help her dye her bangs green for the first time. This is of course a high-risk act—it can go sideways, and it did. Michaela was trying to figure out what went wrong with the dying process and how to make Lou's world right again.

While all this was underway, Bel showed up for a quick twenty-four-hour break from her summer camp counselor job a couple of hours away. She brought two fellow counselors with her. They'd all been working around the clock in the Texas heat. They were sweaty, sleepy, and sweet. We gave them food to eat and pointed them to showers and naps. Later, some of Bel's old high school friends came over, too, and I ended up cooking for everyone late into the evening—very late, as we'd run out of rice for the stir fry and the college kids had to do a mid-cook grocery store run. Finally, around nine, we gathered around our kitchen table with more people than it can fit, and we ate and talked for a long while. Annie, the dog, went from person to person for petting. One of Bel's camp counselor friends, Ellie, has the sharpest, funniest wit you could ever want at a dinner table, and she had us in stitches. At one point, she and Lou were trading barbs, and it was basically everything I could ask for from a kitchen table.

The next morning, I woke up early, went for a run, then came back to fix breakfast. We made crepes, sausage, and scrambled eggs, and soon another one of Bel's friends showed up, then another, and our table was again crowded with people eating and talking until it was time for Bel and her crew to return to camp.

The rest of Sunday was just as full as Friday and Saturday had been. Cleaning for all of us, grad-school work for Michaela, finance stuff for me. Just as I was done with my tasks and ready to zone out on the couch, Lou reminded me that the weekend before, I'd told her we'd have a dad-daughter outing. We used Henry's rented tuxedo return as an excuse to go get ice cream, as if I needed any additional calories. We came back and played Spades for a while. We roasted a chicken and baked some bread. Once Michaela was done with her studies, we gathered around an episode of "Survivor" but paid it little attention because we got into a fervent discussion about how each of us would do on the show. Henry would play a great social game. Michaela said she would, too, but we all disagreed roundly with her. "You have multiple tells," Henry said, and she knew it was true. Lou would crush it because she has no qualms about messing with people. She really, really enjoys it, and she's good at it, and I told her that her ruthlessness would serve her well. Bel would be a wild card, completely unpredictable.

And me? Everyone agreed that I'd be voted off right away. I'd get lost in relationships and lose any sense of strategy, if I even knew how to build one in the first place.

We talked through the whole episode, turned it off, and cleaned the kitchen one last time.

I was so exhausted I could barely get myself to bed.

I'd been bone tired for weeks, months. I'd been feeling defeated by so many things in life. I'd been worried that I'd not built anything lasting. Was anything I was doing working? Was any of it any good? And then that very full weekend fell into our laps, not one I made, but one that was given.

Sometimes you look up and see that everything you need is already here. Sometimes you realize that everything you could ever want in this life is sitting around your kitchen table. The table is a summit. The view is spectacular. You can see the curve of the earth. You're exhausted, and you're grateful.